Clarence Thomas

SUPREME COURT JUSTICE

Muhammad Ali
Maya Angelou
Josephine Baker
George Washington Carver
Ray Charles
Johnnie Cochran
Frederick Douglass
W.E.B. Du Bois
Jamie Foxx
Marcus Garvey
Savion Glover
Alex Haley
Jimi Hendrix
Gregory Hines
Langston Hughes
Jesse Jackson
Scott Joplin
Coretta Scott King
Martin Luther King Jr.
Spike Lee
Malcolm X
Bob Marley
Thurgood Marshall
Barack Obama
Jesse Owens
Rosa Parks
Colin Powell
Condoleezza Rice
Chris Rock
Clarence Thomas
Sojourner Truth
Harriet Tubman
Nat Turner
Madam C.J. Walker
Booker T. Washington
Oprah Winfrey
Tiger Woods

Black Americans of Achievement
LEGACY EDITION

Clarence Thomas

SUPREME COURT JUSTICE

Vicki Cox

CHELSEA HOUSE
PUBLISHERS
An imprint of Infobase Publishing

Clarence Thomas

Copyright © 2008 by Infobase Publishing

Chelsea House
An imprint of Infobase Publishing
132 West 31st Street
New York NY 10001

Library of Congress Cataloging-in-Publication Data
Cox, Vicki.
  Clarence Thomas / by Vicki Cox. — Legacy ed.
      p. cm. — (Black Americans of achievement)
  Includes bibliographical references and index.
  ISBN 978-1-60413-048-5 (hardcover)
  1. Thomas, Clarence, 1948– 2. Judges—United States—Biography. [1. United States.
Supreme Court—Biography. 2. African American judges—Biography.] I. Title. II. Series.
  KF8745.T48C69 2008
  347.73'2634—dc22
  [B]
                                    2008010495

Chelsea House books are available at special discounts when purchased in bulk quantities for businesses, associations, institutions, or sales promotions. Please call our Special Sales Department in New York at (212) 967-8800 or (800) 322-8755.

You can find Chelsea House on the World Wide Web at http://www.chelseahouse.com

Series design by Keith Trego
Composition by Mark Lerner
Cover design by Keith Trego and Jooyoung An
Cover printed by Yurchak Printing, Landisville, Pa.
Book printed and bound by Yurchak Printing, Landisville, Pa.
Printed in the United States of America

This book is printed on acid-free paper.

All links and Web addresses were checked and verified to be correct at the time of publication. Because of the dynamic nature of the Web, some addresses and links may have changed since publication and may no longer be valid.

Contents

Confirmation Hearings

"Thomas!" "Thomas!" "Thomas!" The crowd filled the corridors of the Russell Senate Office Building, chanting Clarence Thomas's name. Policemen and bodyguards wedged into the crowd, making a path for Thomas and his wife, Virginia. Supporters waved. Some reached out to shake his hand, and one woman stepped out of the crowd to hug him. Cameramen, four deep, walked backward in front of him, their cameras' spotlights shining into Clarence Thomas's face. Behind their glare, millions watched as Thomas made his way up the marble staircase toward the Senate Caucus Room.

Although he smiled and nodded at his supporters as they gathered around him, Thomas was not in a good mood. In fact, he was furious. That day, October 12, 1991, had become the defining moment of his life. He was on his way to fight for his reputation, save his confirmation to the Supreme Court, and determine his future. Thomas could just as well have been

All Supreme Court nominees must undergo intensive questioning from the U.S. Senate before they are confirmed. Few, however, can say that their experience was like that of Clarence Thomas. He appears above during his testimony in front of the Senate Judiciary Committee in October 1991, his wife behind him.

walking into Rome's Colosseum. The Caucus Room's Corinthian columns rose two stories to the gilded ceiling, dwarfing the spectators who crowded into it. The U.S. senators inside, ready to question him, could just as well have been lions.

The Senate Caucus Room was jammed with 300 spectators, journalists, and members of Congress who wanted to hear Clarence Thomas speak. Camera lights were strung across the room above him. Photographers squatted, knelt, and stood five deep to Thomas's right, their telephoto lenses trained on the stocky black man who had become the center of a nationwide scandal.

Thomas sat down at the witness table with a microphone in front of him. His wife, dressed in a black and white checkered suit, and Senator John Danforth, his former boss and chief supporter in the Senate, sat behind him.

Thomas faced the 14 members of the Senate Judiciary Committee, who were seated behind a curved table, wearing somber dark suits, white shirts, and intense expressions. In front of each was a clutter of nameplates, microphones, folders, and pads of paper. Senator Joe Biden, the committee chair, banged the gavel three times and called the Senate hearing to order. Behind him hung the United States flag. Senator Edward Kennedy, a Thomas opponent, sat to his left, and Senator Strom Thurmond, a Thomas supporter, sat to his right. The others were spread down the massive desk that dominated much of the room.

Thomas stood, raised his right hand, and swore to tell the truth. Then he sat down. He opened a manila folder and began to read his 16-page statement.

Thomas spoke slowly, looking from one committee member to another. "I have been wracking my brains, and eating my insides out trying to think of what I could have said or done to Anita Hill to lead her to allege that I was interested in her in more than a professional way, and that I talked with her about pornographic or X-rated films," he said, according to John Danforth's book, *Resurrection*.

Thomas's reputation and life was connected to a 35-year-old law professor from the University of Oklahoma because of two words: sexual harassment. That professor, Anita Hill, said that when Thomas was her boss, he had hounded her for dates, described pornographic material to her, and had insisted on talking to her about various sex-related topics.

Such behavior for any person—man or woman—is unthinkable and against the law. Federal law, as later reported in *The New Republic*, described sexual harassment as behavior that "has the purpose or effect of unreasonably interfering with an individual's work performance or creating an intimidating, hostile, or offensive work environment." As head of the Equal Employment Opportunity Commission (EEOC), Thomas had been in charge of investigating and prosecuting individuals or companies who were accused of doing the very things that now threatened to ruin his reputation.

Even more troubling, the words "sexual harassment" had been associated with a man who had just been nominated to the United States Supreme Court. The accusations called into question his morals, his ethics, and his ability to be a good justice.

Thomas had recently testified before the Judiciary Committee for five days, explaining his positions on the Constitution and the law. It was a grueling experience, but everyone believed that the Senate would shortly confirm him to the Supreme Court. Then Hill's accusations sent Washington reeling and shocked the public. Even such historic world events as the crumbling of Communism in the USSR took a backseat to the explosive charges against Thomas.

Detailed accusations of sexual harrassment had never echoed under the four crystal chandeliers or disturbed the dignity of the Senate Caucus Room. These surroundings were usually reserved for more conventional government issues— the sinking of the Titanic, the World War II Defense Program, organized crime, and peace on earth. The major television networks interrupted their programs to televise the testimonies of Thomas and Hill. Experts would later estimate that, at times, 30 million people watched the Clarence Thomas–Anita Hill drama as it unfolded on their screens.

In front of the Judiciary Committee, Thomas spoke slowly. Breaking his statement into short, seven- or eight-word phrases, he paused frequently and pursed or licked his lips. He looked through his black-framed glasses at each committee member. His deep bass voice was firm. His face was strained;

DID YOU KNOW?

The U.S. Constitution established the Supreme Court but said little about how it was to be structured and run. The president nominates candidates to be justices of the Court and then the Senate votes on whether or not to approve them. Justices serve for life; they leave by retiring, dying, or impeachment. The Constitution does not specify the number of justices or what qualifications they should have.

At the Supreme Court's first session in 1790, there were five justices. For most of the following century, the justices were required to "ride circuit" and hold circuit court twice a year in each judicial district. Traveling in slow, bumpy stagecoaches proved exhausting and inefficient, so Congress added two more seats to ensure that the justices would reach all of the circuit courts. It added the eighth and ninth seats in 1837. The number stayed there until 1863, when the Court reached its largest at 10 justices. In 1866, the Republican Congress wanted to prevent Democratic president Andrew Johnson from appointing justices who would comply with his policies, so it passed a law that would eventually reduce the number of seats to seven. Nonetheless, the Judiciary Act of 1869 (also known as the Circuit Judges Act of 1869) again increased the number of seats to nine. When the Supreme Court struck down many of Franklin Delano Roosevelt's policies in the 1930s, Roosevelt tried to "pack" the Court with judges sympathetic to his ideas by increasing the number to 15. He failed, and since then, the number has stayed at nine.

Since the Court was established, there have been 16 chief justices and 108 associate justices (5 of whom went on to become chief justice). The average term of a justice is 16 years. Clarence Thomas has already served more than that average. On average, a new justice is appointed approximately every 22 months.

The qualifications to be a Supreme Court justice have never been defined. Because law schools have not always existed, it was not until 1957 (with the ninety-first justice) that every justice on the Court had a law degree. Experience as a judge has not always been a requirement, either. During the Court's tenure, six chief justices, as well as six associate justices, had not been judges previously. Of the 108 total associate justices, 84 have had less than 10 years of federal or state court experience. Although justices now often come from the Federal Court of Appeals, they have also been U.S. senators, governors, members of the House of Representatives, and law school professors. One, Chief Justice William Howard Taft, was a former president.

his jaw was taut. "I have not said or done the things that Anita Hill has alleged. God has gotten me through . . . and he is my judge," *The Black Scholar* reported Thomas said.

Thomas recalled his relationship with Anita Hill and admitted to being shocked that someone he had considered a friend would suggest that he had done those things. Thomas gave Hill a job at the Department of Education in 1981 as an attorney-adviser. Then she followed him to the Equal Employment Opportunity Commission (EEOC) as a special assistant. In 1983, he recommended her for a teaching position at Oral Roberts Law School.

"I treated her as I treated my other special assistants," Thomas said, according to *The Black Scholar*. "I tried to treat them all cordially, professionally, and respectfully. . . . I had no reason or bias to believe my relationship with Anita Hill was anything but this way until the FBI visited me a little more than two weeks ago."

Then he turned his cold fury on the Judiciary Committee for leaking Hill's charges to the public. He told them of the harm he had suffered and of the hurt done to his family. He criticized the way in which politics had turned the confirmation process into a witch hunt. He told about reporters sneaking into his garage to look through his garbage and about people poking into his divorce papers. He reminded them of the vicious rumors about anti-Semitism, wife beating, and drug use that surfaced during the 103 days after President Bush nominated him. "This is not American," *The Black Scholar* reported that he told them. "This is Kafkaesque. It has got to stop. It must stop for the benefit of future nominees and our country. Enough is enough."

He told them, "I am proud of my life, proud of what I have done, and what I have accomplished, proud of my family, and this process, this process is trying to destroy it all. No job is worth what I have been through, no job. . . . Confirm me if you

Anita Hill's shocking allegations against Thomas caused on uproar, both in the Senate and among the American people. This photograph shows Anita Hill during her testimony to the Senate Judiciary Committee, which took place in the Caucus Room of the Senate Office Building.

want, don't confirm me if you are so led, but let this process end. Let me and my family regain our lives."

Commentators thought that Thomas was about to withdraw from the confirmation process entirely. Of course, if he did that, everyone would conclude that he had done all the things Hill said. If he backed away, he would be ruined, branded as the man who sexually harassed an employee.

Thomas did not withdraw his name. He did not retreat from the scandal. Instead, according to *The Black Scholar*, he told the Judiciary Committee, "Mr. Chairman, I am a victim of this process and my name has been harmed, my integrity has been harmed, my character has been harmed, my family has been harmed, my friends have been harmed. There is nothing this committee, this body or this country can do to give me my good name back, nothing."

The next sentence, reported by *The Black Scholar*, was a hint of the explosive statement he would make later in the day, shocking listeners with a reference to one of the most shameful periods in American history. For a time, whites terrorized African Americans by hanging black men from trees or scaffolds. Such violent acts were scars on the nation's conscience. Thomas brought the past back when he said, "I will not provide the rope for my own lynching, or for further humiliation."

As Thomas read his statement, the room was silent. Aides behind the senators stopped talking and passing notes. Spectators quit rustling papers in the back of the room. Senators on the committee said nothing. According to *Resurrection*, one staffer said, "[I] had never seen in all my years up here a hearing that had such a shocking effect on senators. I have always been struck by the power, the ability of senators to gain the upper hand on any witness. I felt like it was a shock wave in the room. They were stunned."

Senator Danforth later said in *U.S. News and World Report*, "Clarence won this the minute he decided he wasn't going to walk on eggshells . . . what you heard was pure Clarence Thomas."

Unfortunately, the truth was that neither Clarence Thomas nor Anita Hill won in the messy, embarrassing war of words that followed. Both were accomplished people who escaped poverty and racism to become role models for all Americans, black or white. Still, they would be permanently marred by the 21 hours of testimony that followed Thomas's initial statement. Even if they never saw each other again, their names and their lives were forever hyphenated in the Clarence Thomas–Anita Hill affair. They might marry others, their careers might take opposite directions, they might live in other parts of the country. Thomas's rise to the highest court in the land was a more worthwhile story to study, but it would always be connected to a scandalous hearing in the Senate Caucus Room. No matter what he did in the future, his name would be linked with the soft-spoken woman who accused him of doing terrible wrong.

2

Pin Point

Three months earlier, Thomas's advisers had created the "Pin Point strategy." To impress the Senate Judiciary Committee, they decided to stress Thomas's personal success story. They wanted the committee to know about the hard times and poverty into which Thomas had been born and from which he had escaped.

Pin Point, Georgia, is not so much a town as a squatting together of a few hundred people. It is located 10 miles (16 kilometers) south of Savannah on a tiny peninsula. In all, the town is only one mile wide and a mile and a half long. Freed slaves from South Carolina and Georgia near the Moon River first settled the town. These freed slaves collectively came to be known as "Gullah" because of their unique way of speaking and their emphasis on their African heritage. Many of the Gullah people who settled in Georgia were called "Geechee," probably because of their proximity to the Little Ogeechee River.

The residents made little money. They spent most of their lives trying to keep food on their tables and clothes on their backs. What income was available came from the nearby oyster factory. The men harvested oysters, crabs, and fish and worked at odd jobs and construction. Young people had a difficult time getting past high school because they were needed to help bring in money for the family. Leola, Thomas's mother, started picking crabs and shucking oysters when she was 9 years old. She earned five cents per pound picked or shucked.

Rather than patronizing a grocery store, residents depended on themselves for food. They grew okra, collard greens,

DID YOU KNOW?

As a young boy, Clarence Thomas spoke a dialect of English called Gullah or Geechee. Its roots lie in a mixture of British English of the eighteenth and nineteenth centuries and African dialects spoken by slaves who were brought to North Carolina, South Carolina, Georgia, and Florida. The dialect was concentrated in an area ranging from Jacksonville, North Carolina, to Jacksonville, Florida, and about 100 miles (161 kilometers) inland. People who lived in Georgia were often called Geechee; those who lived in South Carolina were called Gullah.

The people who spoke this dialect lived near the coast and on islands that were separated from the mainland. At first, mainlanders avoided the area because of fear of tropical fevers. Gullah/Geechee people traveled from their homes to the mainland by boat but eventually decided that they preferred to live quietly on the islands using the traditions, foods, religion, and beliefs of their West African beginnings.

As a point of comparison, in English, Psalm 23 from the New Testament says, "The Lord is my Shepherd. I shall not want." In Gullah/Geechee it is written, "De Lawd me shephud. A hab ebrytin wa A need."

Today, only about 10,000 people speak Gullah/Geechee as a primary language; another 250,000 use its words from time to time. In 2006, Congress passed the Gullah/Geechee Cultural Heritage Corridor Act, earmarking $10 million over 10 years to go toward the preservation and interpretation of historic sites that relate to the Gullah/Geechee culture.

tomatoes, and corn. They trapped and ate raccoons and opossums, and they caught fish, shrimp, and oysters.

One positive thing about living in Pin Point was that neighbors were close, physically and emotionally. Many were related. They had no locks on their doors, they picnicked together often, and they gave each other nicknames. Leola, Thomas's mother, was "Pigeon" because her toes turned in. Others were "Pig," "Bubba," and "Nerve." Clarence became "Boy," and his brother, Myers, became "Peanut," even though he weighed 13 pounds at birth (the average is about 7 pounds).

Clarence's father was M.C. Thomas. M.C. dropped out of school in fifth grade and lived with his family on the grounds of the Bethesda Home for Boys, one of the oldest orphanages in the country. He helped his father grow crops to feed the white boys who lived there.

Clarence's mother was Leola Williams. She lived with her aunt after her mother died. Leola Williams's father, Myers Anderson, lived close by in Savannah but had little to do with his illegitimate daughter. The first time she saw him was when she was 12 years old, when she attended the funeral of a sister she never knew.

Forbidden to attend dances by her aunt, Leola often went to bed fully clothed and then sneaked out the window when her aunt was asleep. On one such adventure, she met M.C. Thomas. She got pregnant at 16; M.C. was 15. The Baptist Church expelled her because of it, and she dropped out of tenth grade. Although Leola's father had fathered two daughters without marrying their mothers, he insisted that the couple marry. Two months after Clarence Thomas's older sister, Emma Mae, was born in November 1946, M.C. and Leola married. Clarence arrived two years after that, and Myers came 16 months later.

ENTER CLARENCE THOMAS
Clarence Thomas was born June 23, 1948, in a shack with no bathroom and no running water. His home was not a very

Above is a 1991 photograph of the house where Leola Williams, Clarence Thomas's mother, lived. When Thomas and his siblings were children, Williams worked as a live-in maid in order to support them; this sometimes meant that the children had to live with other relatives in the family.

nice place to live. Water was carried through the woods in buckets from a nearby faucet. Some was stored in a washtub for bathing, and some was put in a bucket to drink with a dipper. Rain, caught in a barrel at the corner of the house, provided water for washing clothing. "In the wintertime, we plugged up the cracks and holes in the walls with old newspapers," Thomas recalled in his autobiography, *My Grandfather's Son.*

After Clarence was born, his mother went back to work at A.S. Varn & Son, the oyster and crab company. With no babysitter available, she sometimes put him in a playpen near the cannery so that she and other workers could keep an eye on him. Leola was a blue-ribbon crab picker. "I could do 75 pounds if I sat there all day," she recalled in Norman Macht's *Clarence Thomas: Supreme Court Justice.* "When I was pregnant with Clarence, I would go home and lie down for a while, then I'd go back and still beat them all."

His parents divorced when he was two years old, just before his little brother, Myers, was born. His father told the judge that Leola neglected their three children and asked the court to give custody to Leola's aunt. Leola remembered things differently. She said that M.C. got another woman pregnant, and the girl's father threatened to shoot M.C. if he did not marry her. Whatever the reason, Thomas's parents split up. M.C. moved away, first to Savannah and then to Philadelphia, leaving Leola to support three children. Clarence Thomas did not know his father. He remembers seeing his father for the first time when he was nine years old and then again when he graduated from high school.

In March 1951, the court awarded custody of the three children to Leola's aunt Annie. Leola worked as a maid in Savannah, returning to Pin Point to see her kids on the weekends. Thomas wrote in his autobiography, "Nothing about my childhood seemed unusual to me at the time. I had no idea that any other life was possible, at least for me." He had only two store-bought toys, a red wagon and a fire truck. Mostly, he and his brother made their own fun: carving watermelon rinds into boats, wrapping moss with aluminum foil to make a ball, and swinging on grapevines like Tarzan.

He testified during his confirmation hearings, "As kids, we caught minnows in the creeks, fiddler crabs in the marshes . . . and skipped shells across the water." Later, he wrote in his autobiography, "We played with 'trains' made out of empty juice cans strung together with old coat hangers and weighted with sand. . . ." Sometimes, he and Myers crammed themselves into an abandoned car tire and rolled down the road. He told Steve Kroft on CBS's *60 Minutes*, "This is what we did. I mean kids today have video games. This is what we spent our time doin'."

On the dirt road in back of the house, a small cinder-block building was the meeting hall for the Brotherhood of Friendship Society. Thurgood Marshall, before he was the Supreme

Court justice who Thomas was nominated to replace, once stopped to speak there as he traveled through the South crusading against segregation.

When Clarence was five or six, his great-aunt, Maggie Devoe, taught him to read from books that her husband brought home from his job working for two white families. Clarence really liked books. Sometimes he would read instead of playing outside with his friends.

In 1954, Clarence put on shoes for the first time. Dressed in hand-me-down clothes from the local Baptist church, he boarded the bus to go to school. That same year, the Supreme Court outlawed segregation in public schools. Georgia, however, ignored the order to desegregate. "I knew nothing of *Brown v. Board of Education*," Thomas wrote in his autobiography. "I was too young to understand such things."

Traditionally, the state and/or school districts did not give the same amount of funding to all-black schools as to it did all-white ones. Black students went to school in rundown buildings, studied from too few worn-out and outdated textbooks, and did without sports equipment, school lunches, and after-school programs.

Clarence attended Haven Home School. Like many other black schools, it was so crowded that he could only attend part of the day. One day, halfway through his first term, Clarence returned home to find that his aunt's house had been destroyed by fire. With everyone else gone, Myers had slipped back home from his uncle's house. He and his cousin tried to light a stove heater. A curtain caught fire, and the wooden shack, with its newspaper insulation, burned to the ground.

"We lost everything," Thomas's mother recalled in Merida and Fletcher's *Supreme Discomfort*. "I don't even have a baby picture of Clarence or me or my other two children because everything was burned up."

Although Thomas's advisers at his confirmation hearing sought to spotlight his life in Pin Point, his critics pointed out that, in reality, Thomas spent only a few years of his childhood there. But his life in the following years would not be much better.

SAVANNAH

Homeless, Thomas's mother left his sister with Aunt Annie, who went to live with another family member in Pin Point, and took Clarence and Myers to Savannah, where she kept house for a man who drove a potato chip truck.

"When I was a boy," Thomas wrote in his autobiography, "Savannah was hell. Overnight I moved from the comparative safety and cleanliness of rural poverty to the foulest kind of urban squalor." The three Thomases lived in a one-room apartment in a slum neighborhood. Leola and Myers shared the only bed; Clarence slept in a chair. They could not afford kerosene to

John Marshall (Chief Justice 1801–1835)

Early on, no one thought that the Supreme Court was supreme at all. Created in 1789, it held only a single two-hour session in its first year and then adjourned. No one submitted any cases. No one thought being a Supreme Court justice was special, either.

John Marshall, the Court's fourth chief justice, changed all that. He established its most important powers: the ability to overturn laws passed by Congress and the concept of using the Constitution as law. The case that established this power, called "judicial review," was *Marbury v. Madison.* It began as dirty politics.

When President John Adams, a Federalist, ran for reelection in 1800, he lost to Thomas Jefferson, a Republican. Out of spite, Adams appointed John Marshall as chief justice and hundreds of other Federalists to judgeships just before the Republicans took over the government; however, 17 appointments, signed and sealed, were not delivered before he left office. Just as spitefully, Jefferson, a Republican, ignored the 17 undelivered appointments. William Marbury, who should have become a justice of the peace based on Adams's appointment, asked the Supreme Court to force Jefferson to award his commission, arguing that Congress had given the light the stove, and food was scarce. "It was cold in the winter," Thomas told CBS's *60 Minutes* correspondent, Steve Kroft. "I mean it was one of the most miserable times of my early life."

Three other tenants lived in the building; they all used the same kitchen, which had an unreliable gas stove and no refrigerator. Worn linoleum covered a dirt floor. The toilet was outside in the backyard, but the bowl was cracked and the wooden seat was rotten. Sometimes raw sewage escaped from the sewer line. Leola had the boys use a chamber pot in their apartment, and Clarence was supposed to empty it on Saturday mornings. "One day I tripped and tumbled all the way down the stairs, landing in a heap at the bottom," Thomas recalled in his autobiography. "The brimming pot followed, drenching me in stale urine."

His mother enrolled Clarence in Savannah's all-black Florance Street School. Like the school in Pin Point, it was so

Court the power to do so with the Judiciary Act of 1789. The Republican Congress was so angry that it passed a law that sent the Supreme Court home for 14 months.

Chief Justice Marshall was in a bad spot. If the Court did not act, it would lose respect. If it ordered Jefferson to give Marbury his commission, the president would refuse and no one would respect the Court, either.

When the Court reconvened, Marshall outsmarted everyone. He stated that Jefferson should have delivered the commission but that the Supreme Court could not tell the president what to do because the Judiciary Act of 1789 was unconstitutional. Jefferson would either have to obey the ruling or allow the Federalists he hated into the court system.

This was the very first time the Supreme Court overturned an act of Congress. By doing so, it turned the Constitution—which had been simply a political statement—into law and gave itself the power to interpret it. It established that the Court would only decide cases that involved constitutional issues. In other words, Marshall and his justices made the Court supreme. Judicial review became the Court's most important power, and it was John Marshall, not the Constitution, who created it.

crowded that children could only attend half a day. Each day, Leola left early in the morning with Myers. Six-year-old Clarence was on his own until it was time for school in the afternoon. In the mornings, he roamed the streets unsupervised. Sometimes, bored with his lessons, he didn't bother to show up school at all.

Later in the summer, the trio moved to a better apartment with a stove and refrigerator in the kitchen and a working outdoor toilet. Clarence even had his own bed.

In 1955, Leola remarried and the family moved across town to a better house: The toilet was still outside, but at least it wasn't broken. Leola's new husband was hardly a footnote in Clarence's life. One biographer said that he did not want the boys around. Another said that he was willing to raise the boys, but Leola did not want any man outside her family to take care of them. Leola told Ken Foskett in *Judging Thomas,* "I couldn't afford a baby-sitter. I didn't want my kids on the street." With school dismissed for summer vacation, Leola turned to the only person left to help her—her father.

She asked Myers Anderson to take the boys to live with him. His response was just one word: "No." Then Leola's stepmother, Christine, spoke up. She threatened to kick Anderson out, saying, "you better pack your clothes," reported Ken Foskett in *Judging Thomas.* "These are my grandchildren, and I plan to take them." Anderson walked away from the conversation without saying anything. When he returned, without a word, the matter was settled.

One Saturday morning, Clarence and Myers Thomas put everything they owned into two brown paper grocery bags. They walked two and a half blocks to their grandparents' home, a journey that sent their lives away from dirt-hard poverty toward a very different life.

3

Tough Love

Myers Anderson's rigid rules, uncompromising expectations, and tough love molded what Clarence Thomas would become and what he would think. Thomas's grandfather was a muscular man with work-hardened hands, a pencil-thin mustache, and a frown that could make a child's whine die in his mouth. "He could make me cry just by looking at me," Thomas's mother later told Ken Foskett in *Judging Thomas.*

Life with Anderson in Savannah was very different from life in Pin Point. Anderson owned his own business and both a car and a truck. His six-room house had things the boys had never seen before, including a freezer, hot water heater, and a washing machine. The flush of his indoor toilet, the first they had ever seen, fascinated Clarence and Myers. They shared a room, but each had his own bed. Clarence had plenty to eat, enough clothes, and even some spending money. His Christmases with

Clarence Thomas and his brother were sent to live with their maternal grandfather, Myers Anderson, in 1955. Anderson, pictured above, dropped out of elementary school in order to work, but he knew the importance of education for his grandsons and saw to it that they studied hard and learned to work hard.

his grandfather included a store-bought set of electric trains and a bright red Western Flyer bicycle.

Anderson had never had a conventional childhood or education. He was the result of an affair between a married Baptist preacher and a young maid. He barely knew his father, and his mother died when he was 9 years old. He then lived with his grandmother, who had been freed from slavery during General Sherman's famous march to the sea. When she died, a teenaged Anderson lived with a no-nonsense uncle whose independence and hard work set the pattern for Anderson's ideas of raising his grandsons. Uncle Charlie started work before daylight and returned home after dark. Children provided more hands for the field or the plow to help out. He did not tolerate horsing around and dealt with it quickly.

Anderson dropped out of school to work before he could read well or use numbers. He depended on his wife, Tina, Clarence's grandmother, to help him. Thomas wrote in *My Grandfather's Son*, "By the time I was in third grade, I was the best reader in the house."

As a young man, Anderson went to Savannah to work for three dollars per week. In the mid 1950s, a white worker stole a nice watch that Anderson was wearing. Disgusted with the white people he encountered, Anderson declared, "I'm going into business for myself," according to a 1991 *Newsweek* article. To sell and haul firewood, he fashioned a truck by sawing off the top of his Model T. He hauled ice in the summer and kerosene and coal in the winter. Later, he delivered heating oil in a tanker truck with "Anderson Fuel Oil Co." painted on the sides.

Anderson taught himself plumbing, bricklaying, and carpentry. "He was one of the smartest men without an education that you've ever seen," his business partner told the authors of *Supreme Discomfort*.

Meyers survived being black in the Deep South by working hard and depending only on himself. Responsible for his grandsons, he intended that they would survive as well. From the first day they arrived in his house, Anderson kept a close eye on "Boy" and "Peanut."

"Daddy didn't whip us regularly," Thomas remembered in his autobiography. "But our encounters with his belt or a switch were far from infrequent, and it soon became clear that he meant to control every aspect of our lives."

Anderson woke the boys up before dawn. They washed and waxed the oil truck, cleaned the car, and cut the grass. On Saturdays, he took them to the lumberyard. While he searched for lumber to recycle, the boys pounded nails out of the boards for recycling, too.

Not even bath time escaped Anderson's eagle eye. He saw to it that the boys used laundry detergent instead of soap, very little water, and washcloths instead of towels for drying off. "Whenever he thought we hadn't gotten ourselves clean enough, he finished the job himself, a terrifying experience that we did everything we could to avoid," Thomas recalled in *My Grandfather's Son*.

By the fourth grade, Thomas was helping Anderson with his oil deliveries. On the one hand, Thomas remembers Anderson explaining that he had taken the heater out of the truck because "the warmth . . . would only make us lazy. . . ." On the other hand, he also watched his grandfather fill oil tanks for people who could not pay him because Anderson could not stand for them to be cold.

In 1957, Anderson decided that he and the boys would build a house in Liberty County, 19 miles (31 kilometers) away. The family stayed there every summer for 10 years. This was Anderson's way of keeping the boys out of trouble during summer vacation. In the 100-degree heat, they plowed, hoed, planted seed, cut sugarcane, and strung barbed-wire fence around Anderson's 72 acres of land. They tended the garden and gathered vegetables to give to the less fortunate. They killed chickens by wringing their necks, dipped them in hot water, and plucked off their feathers. They scraped the hair off slaughtered hogs. They skinned the deer, raccoons, or squirrels that Anderson shot. He woke them up at 4:00 A.M. to clean his fish. In a *60 Minutes* interview Thomas told correspondent Steve Kroft, "If you want to be pleasant about it, you can call us field hands. But we were his laborers. I got up the nerve and said, 'Daddy, you know, slavery's over.' And he said, 'Not in my damn house.'"

"I was glad he wasn't my grandfather," said Robert DeShay, Thomas's childhood friend in a 1991 *Newsweek* article. "He used to work Clarence like a dog."

As a child, Thomas seethed under his grandfather's heavy hand, but as an adult, he has defended what Anderson did as necessary. "There's a difference between someone who's 'harsh' and someone who is 'hard,'" he told Rush Limbaugh in a 2007 interview. "You lived in the South, as my grandparents did, and you had to survive . . . he had to become a hard man, with very hard rules, very hard discipline for himself. . . . But that is quite different from being harsh."

Although Anderson would not allow himself to hug or praise his young charges, their grandmother, whom they called Aunt Tina, was anything but hard or harsh. She made them sweet potato pie, greens, and fried chicken, and she wouldn't allow anyone to touch Thomas's drumstick. "If I was there at supper time," Thomas's mother, Leola Williams, recalled in Macht's biography, "I could sit in any chair but her boys' chairs. And I better not touch the pieces of chicken that were the boys' favorites."

Myers Anderson fenced his young charges in with his own values: hard work, discipline, and education. He didn't want them anywhere near where they could get in trouble. In Savannah, he wouldn't allow the teenaged boys to go to dances and required them to be home by the time the streetlights came on—even on weekends.

The one place Anderson did allow Thomas to go was Savannah's Carnegie Library. The two-story brick building for blacks was just three blocks from Anderson's house. Its basement provided escape from Anderson's stern glare and unending lectures and from Savannah's summer heat. "I used to run to the library to flip through the pages and dream," Thomas later said, according to David Kaplan in *Newsweek*.

At age seven, he listened as the librarians read stories. Later, he leafed through "every single page of every single encyclopedia," the authors of *Supreme Discomfort* reported. "I was never prouder than when I got my first library card, though the day when I'd checked out enough books to fill it up came close," Thomas wrote in *His Grandfather's Son.*

In the library's adult section, he discovered C.S. Forester's Captain Horatio Hornblower. "I didn't like the water myself," he said, "but reading about how they handled the ships during storms, and all their adventures out on the ocean . . . took me out of that segregated library in the segregated South."

Clarence also loved comic books like *The Rawhide Kid*, *Kid Colt*, *Superman*, *Spider-Man*, and *The Green Lantern.* When Anderson let him watch television, Clarence enjoyed Western series such as *The Roy Rogers Show* and *Sky King.*

Clarence learned a great deal from observing the example that his grandfather set and following his stern instructions. As an adult, Thomas would emulate his grandfather's self-

Thurgood Marshall (Associate Justice 1967–1991)

Thurgood Marshall was the first black Supreme Court justice. Marshall was the grandson of a slave. His real name was Thoroughgood, but in second grade he changed it to Thurgood. It stuck.

As a lawyer, particularly as Chief Counsel for the NAACP, he specialized in segregation issues, especially in schools. Marshall won 29 of the 32 cases he argued in front of the Supreme Court.

His most important case was 1951's *Brown v. Board of Education.* Seven-year-old Linda Brown attended an all-black school more than a mile from her house when there was an all-white school just three blocks away. To get to her school, she walked through dangerous railroad yards, rode on a public bus, and waited 30 minutes outside before school started. Her father tried, unsuccessfully, to enroll her in the nearby all-white school. When that effort failed, 13 other parents, representing 20 children, joined the suit that Brown brought against the Topeka, Kansas, school district. Marshall was the lawyer for the group.

The Supreme Court, headed by Chief Justice Earl Warren, unanimously ruled that segregation in public schools was unconstitutional. What impressed the Court was Marshall's use of the "Brandeis Brief," which gave

discipline, willingness to work hard, and toughness. Relying only on himself, Thomas would learn to form his own ideas independent of others' opinions.

ST. BENEDICT THE MOOR SCHOOL

In 1955, Myers Anderson, a Roman Catholic by faith, paid a fee between $25 and $30 annual tuition for Clarence and Myers to enroll in St. Benedict the Moor School.

The Franciscan nuns thought that Thomas had missed too much school the year before, but they reluctantly put him in second grade. Anderson bought the boys their school uniforms: ties, white shirts, blue pants, and sweaters. Then he laid down the rules. According to Macht's biography, he said, "Your teachers are always right. Your grandmother's always right. If

data to explain how segregated schools harmed black children.

Despite his standing in the black community, Marshall had a difficult time getting confirmed to the Supreme Court in 1967. Newspapers thought that he was unqualified and charged that he was not even the best black candidate. One printed that he had a reputation for "laziness." Although the three previous nominees had been confirmed in less than two weeks each, Marshall waited for more than two months. In the end, the vote to confirm him was 69–11; 20 senators refused to vote. Marshall asked Justice Hugo Black, a former member of the Klu Klux Klan, to swear him in.

The liberal Marshall believed that integration was the key to racial equality. He supported school busing, a woman's right to an abortion, affirmative action, abolition of the death penalty, and expanded prisoner rights. He was also a strong supporter of First Amendment rights. He once stated, "If the First Amendment means anything, it means that a state has no business telling a man, sitting alone in his own house, what books he may read or what films he may watch."

Marshall was a justice for 24 years. When he retired, Clarence Thomas was nominated to take his place.

they beat you in school and you come home and complain about it, you'll get another one."

Missing school was also unacceptable. Anderson told Clarence and Myers that, if they died, he would take them to school for three days just to be sure they weren't faking. Clarence paid attention and was not absent or tardy.

It was just a short walk between Anderson's rules at home and the nuns' intense, tough love at school. Students had to sit up straight, raise their hands to speak, and speak only when spoken to. Anyone who strayed from the rules got whacked across the palm with a stick or a ruler.

Jim Crow laws permitted others to refuse Aunt Tina the use of a restroom. They prevented black and white basketball teams from playing together and black children from setting foot on a Georgia beach. The Irish nuns had not grown up with the South's racism, however. They concerned themselves with the person within the skin that others despised. According to Macht's biography, at a reunion 20 years later, Thomas paid tribute to the nuns "who made me pray when I didn't want to and didn't know why I should—who made me work when I saw no reason to—who made me believe in the equality of races when our country paid lip service to equality and our church tolerated inequality—who made me accept responsibility for my own acts when I looked for excuses. . . . Without our nuns, I would not have made it to square one."

Between the nuns at school and his grandfather at home, Clarence was squeezed everywhere by adult expectations. He had no place else to go but up. His grades improved from Cs in second grade to Bs in third grade. By eighth grade, he was a straight-A student. He was not the smartest student in class, so he worked hard for everything he got. "He was always about business," a classmate told Ken Foskett. "I think he was focused from day one."

Clarence excelled in other areas as well. At 8 years old, he studied to be an altar boy, memorizing the Latin phrases in order to assist the priest. At 13, he was named altar boy of the year. Clarence also earned the right to fold the flag when it came off the flagpole and was named a patrol boy.

Clarence was not perfect, though. Once, he and two friends perched on a fire escape so they could dump a bag of sand on a priest standing below. After school, he and Myers would climb into an open boxcar when a freight train slowed for a crossing. Then, as the train picked up speed, they would leap off—something that would have horrified both his grandparents and railroad officials.

Clarence loved sports, although his grandfather would not let him play much. The brothers made their own basketball hoops, nailing trash cans (with the bottoms rusted out) to a pole. The basketballs were, according to Thomas's autobiography, leaky and lopsided. "This made it hard to dribble," he wrote, "but that didn't matter, since the dirt lane on which we played was covered with rocks, glass, nails, and other debris."

Because Clarence dribbled between his legs and behind his back, the other kids started to call him "Couze," after Bob Cousy, his favorite Boston Celtics star. They also called him "the Black Hole" because once Clarence got the ball, no one else could touch it. In addition to basketball, Thomas remembered playing with hula-hoops, yo-yos, marbles, and jacks, and tinkering with his bicycle. He and his friends also played a version of stickball.

At the time, dark skin color was definitely not considered beautiful. The lighter the skin, the straighter the hair, the narrower bone structure, the better. Thomas's skin was very black, his nose was broad, his hair was curly, and his lips were wide. According to Ken Foskett's biography, Thomas once said, "The reality was the more Negroid you were the more you got it. So me, I'm Negroid, I took my hits."

As an adult, Thomas bitterly remembered his nickname, "ABC: America's Blackest Child." Some of his classmates recall that the dark-skinned Clarence did not fit in, but others remember him as a kid with a positive reputation. Others recall that, instead of Clarence being singled out, everyone picked on everybody else. A former classmate of Thomas's, Marion Poole, said that she was called "Bony Marony" because she was so skinny.

Clarence, all of five foot two inches tall and 98 pounds, graduated from St. Benedict in 1962 and enrolled in the all-black St. Pius X High School. The nuns there were more demanding than those at his old school. Clarence responded, studying until 9:00 P.M. at the library and then putting in another two hours at the kitchen table before bedtime.

Clarence joined the newspaper staff during his sophomore year and briefly considered becoming a journalist. After visiting St. John Vianny Minor Seminary, however, his interest turned to the religious life. That year, as Clarence was beginning to contemplate his future, President Lyndon B. Johnson signed the Civil Rights Act of 1964, which created a new agency, the Equal Employment Opportunity Commission. Though he did not know it, Clarence would one day be its chairman.

Clarence told his grandfather that he wanted to become a priest. The $400 annual tuition that the seminary required was a lot of money for a man who earned barely $7,000 per year, but Anderson agreed to pay it on one condition: "If you go, you have to stay. You can't quit," Thomas remembered his grandfather saying in *My Grandfather's Son*. "He gave me his blessing, then added, 'Don't shame me—and don't shame our race.'" Little did Clarence know that that promise would be the most important one he would not keep.

4

Seminary Life

One Sunday in September 1964, Myers Anderson brought Clarence to St. John Vianney Minor Seminary, where he joined 21 other sophomores. The boarding school for boys, about 6 miles (10 kilometers) outside Savannah, was not very impressive. Two yellow, single-story cinder-block buildings held classrooms, dorms, and a dining room. The church, resting on cinder blocks, had a stumpy steeple and plain windows; its only outstanding feature was the oak trees that towered over it. A statue of Saint John Vianney, the patron saint of parish priests, stood in the center of the courtyard.

Thomas stepped into a new world, much different from his life in Savannah. His new room—a dormitory—was very different from the one he had shared with his brother. At the seminary, narrow metal beds alternated with small bureaus; some were lined up along the walls, and others filled the middle of the room. The people there were different, too. Instead of being just one of many black students, Thomas was one black surrounded by white faces. "I thought they were all staring at me," he wrote in his autobiography. "I wanted to turn right around and go back home, but it was too late."

Religion punctuated Thomas's daily schedule. He awoke at 6:00 A.M. Prayers and morning Mass began at 6:30. Lunch was preceded by a recitation of the Rosary, and prayers were completed before lights out at 10:00 P.M. Students spent Good Friday and Easter in the chapel, where they prayed on their knees for four hours.

Thomas's assignments and homework were more difficult than he was used to, and he worried that his abilities might not be equal to those of his white classmates. Because he had not yet taken the Latin courses that he would need to get into a major seminary, Thomas was placed back in the tenth grade. He wrote in *My Grandfather's Son*, "The panic I felt on my first day gave way to a constant state of controlled anxiety." His grandfather had taught him not to be afraid of hard work, though, and Thomas buckled down and improved his study habits.

Thomas's chief instructor was a demanding priest, Father William Coleman. Students received an automatic zero if they came to his class unprepared. In *Judging Thomas*, Foskett reported that Coleman once gave a student a 99 instead of the 100 he had earned on a Latin exam, explaining that "nobody was perfect." Early on, he trampled over Thomas's sensitivity of being black in a white world. During his first semester, the priest called Thomas into his office and declared that Thomas had to lose his Gullah/Geechee dialect if he expected to get anywhere. He announced that he would tutor Thomas until he could speak standard English. "His blunt words hit me like a slap in the face: I thought he was saying that I was inferior because I was black," Thomas later wrote in his autobiography. "Years later I found out that he'd said similar things to white students whose accents were about as thick as mine—but his

This photograph was taken from the 1967 edition of *The Grail*, the yearbook of St. John Vianney Minor Seminary. It features Clarence Thomas in his position as business editor of the 1967 *Grail* staff.

candor hurt me, and it also made me self-conscious about talking out loud in class."

Being six miles from Savannah, Thomas found some breathing room from his grandfather, who had nicknamed the cocky 16-year-old "Mr. Know-It-All." Although Thomas was willing to form his entire life around his grandfather's dream of him becoming Savannah's first black priest, he was not willing to sacrifice playing sports at school. At last, he was a star. "He was the best athlete in the school," a former classmate told the authors of *Supreme Discomfort*. "Without a doubt. . . . He was strong as an ox and fast as lightning." Playing quarterback, Thomas led his eight-man football team, the Cowboys, to the school championship. His forward pass could literally knock a receiver down. Thomas was also the captain and leading scorer of the school basketball team. He dunked the basketball and led fast breaks. Merida and Fletcher reported that the school newspaper praised his "superb throwing" and "elusive footwork." It called him "faster than a speedy spitball . . . more powerful than home brew" on the basketball court.

Outwardly, Thomas seemed to fit into the white world of St. John's. "He was essentially one of the guys, as far as I was concerned," said Steve Seyfried, who co-edited the school newspaper with Thomas. Even Richard Chisholm, St. John's only other black student, remembered in *Supreme Discomfort* that Thomas was outgoing and confident with a "jovial disposition about him . . . so it was hard to know if he was experiencing the same things."

The "things" Chisholm referred to were incidents and comments that arose from their white classmates' casual racism. Having grown up thinking themselves superior to blacks, they were unaware that their manners and their conversation were laced with putdowns. They did not have a clue that writing "Clarence, you did very well in spite of being black" was hurtful. Such comments cut like a razor. One night, in the darkened dorm room, one boy yelled out, "Smile, Clarence, so we can see you." Thomas has retold that story many times in his speeches. What upset him the most was the silence that followed. None of his friends stood up for him or even said, "Shut up." In another incident, Thomas made a basket, earning the right to choose the teams for a pick-up game. He was stunned when the players walked to the other end of the court and began to play without him. In his autobiography, Thomas remembered that painful moment: "I walked back alone to the seminary building, wondering whether they were laughing at me behind my back. . . . Every step was agony. As soon as I got to the building, I went straight to the chapel to pray."

Another time, someone broke the head off the statue of St. Jude that Thomas won in a Latin spelling bee. He glued the head back on, only to discover it broken—again. He glued it back on—another time. "Whoever was breaking it must have gotten the message: I'd keep gluing it forever if I needed to. I wasn't giving up," he wrote *in My Grandfather's Son*.

Thomas did not seem to completely belong to either the white world at the seminary or in black society back in Savannah. "I was a stray dog," he said in *Supreme Discomfort*. Thomas remembered in his autobiography that a white student wrote in his sophomore yearbook, "Keep on trying, Clarence. Someday you'll be as good as us." Yet his black friends in Savannah teased him about going to the white school, "St. John's the Cemetery," and made fun of his increasingly more educated way of speaking. In a 1984 *Legal Times* interview, Thomas reflected, "We're a mixed-up generation, those of us who were sent out to integrate society."

In 1965, a year after Thomas started at St. John's, riots erupted in Watts, a predominantly black neighborhood in Los Angeles. Halfway across the country, 34 people died and property damage totaled $40 million. At the time, Thomas was undergoing his own racial crisis. He could not understand how his classmates, who were studying to be priests and dedicating their lives to God, could be so bigoted. It was a dilemma that he struggled to solve.

In *Supreme Discomfort*, Merida and Fletcher recorded an often-quoted column that Thomas wrote as co-editor of St. John's newspaper: "I think races would fare better if extremists would crawl back into their holes, and let the people, whom this will really affect, do just a little thinking for themselves. . . . It's about time for the average American to rise from his easy chair and do what he really and truly believes God demands of him—time to peel off the veil of hate and contempt, and don the cloak of love (black for white and white for black)."

Hugo Black (Associate Justice 1937–1971)

President Franklin D. Roosevelt nominated Hugo Black to be an associate justice of the Supreme Court in 1937. There was a great deal of criticism over the nomination. The *Washington Post* criticized Black's "lack of training" and "extreme partisanship." True, he did not graduate from high school before going on to medical, liberal arts, and law schools. True, as senator, he had worked hard to get the number of Supreme Court justices expanded from 9 to 15, as President Roosevelt wanted. The *Chicago Tribune* declared that Roosevelt had picked "the worst he could find." Another paper called Black "a vulgar dog."

Black was confirmed anyway. Then, a Pennsylvania newspaper broke a shocking story: Black had been a member of the Ku Klux Klan. In a radio address, Black admitted to joining the KKK in 1923, marching in parades, making speeches at meetings, and wearing the robes and hood of the organization. He said, "Ladies and gentlemen, an effort is being made to convince the people of America that I am intolerant, and I am prejudiced. I number among my friends many numbers of the colored race. Certainly they are entitled to the full measure of protection afforded by the Constitution and our laws. I did join the Klan. I later resigned. I never rejoined." His sincerity and passion swung public support his way, and he was not forced to resign.

Black may have been in the KKK for 2 years, but during his 34 years on the Court, he proved to be a champion of minorities, civil rights, and civil liberties. He was so hated by whites in the South that any visit there endangered his life. Black voted in favor of giving accused criminals rights that are now considered entirely natural: the right to remain silent and the right to an attorney (and to have the state provide one if they cannot afford counsel), something the poor had not always enjoyed. Like John Marshall, he was a strong defender of the freedom of speech. The plain-speaking Black said, "Freedom of speech means that you shall not do something to people either for the views they express, or the words they speak or write."

This image, from the yearbook *The Grail*, shows the 1967 graduating class, which included Clarence Thomas (center, back row). In his last year at the seminary, Thomas was co-editor of *The Pioneer*, the school newsletter.

During the summer after his sophomore year, Thomas took on new personal challenges. He taught himself to type using an old typewriter that one of the nuns had given him. He said, "I spent what free time I had teaching myself first-year algebra and reading at least five pages of a difficult book every day, underlining all the unfamiliar words and looking them up." He finally figured out the value of good study habits and self-discipline. The hard work paid off with top-notch grades the following year. One classmate jokingly wrote in his yearbook that year, "blew that test, only a 98."

MISSOURI SEMINARY

Thomas graduated from St. John's in 1967. In the continuing pursuit of his goal of becoming a priest, he boarded a train from Savannah to Atlanta with a shoebox filled with Aunt Tina's fried chicken, boiled eggs, white bread, and pound cake. He was off to enter Immaculate Conception Seminary. On the way, he stopped in Atlanta, where he rode in glass elevators for the first time. Then, to get to Kansas City, Missouri, he took his first plane ride.

Immaculate Conception Seminary, in northwestern Missouri, was a quiet place, 20 miles (32 kilometers) from Maryville, the nearest town. The seminary had a church, academic buildings, dormitories, a post office, a print shop for selling greeting cards, and a reservoir with fish. Though Thomas had been the only black student at St. John's, now he was one of 4 blacks in the freshman class of 64 students, which included 6 of his St. John's classmates.

At Conception, Thomas bought a cassock and a Roman collar for prayers and Mass. "I . . . loved the formality (and novelty) of wearing them," he wrote in his autobiography. "The same way I'd loved my school uniforms. For a brief time, it seemed that my vocation was becoming more real . . . that I was no longer playing out a young boy's dreams."

His classmates at Immaculate Conception recalled Thomas as a hard-working, disciplined student, and a good athlete. Thomas, however, called every day "pricked by prejudice," inside the world where love and kindness were supposed to be the rules. His first roommate jokingly opened a knife when Thomas first walked in the room, and Thomas did not receive a trophy, the typical reward, the year that he was named outstanding athlete. With all the racial unrest going on outside the seminary, Thomas continued to question the Catholic Church's position on the treatment of blacks. "The Church remained silent, and its silence haunted me," he wrote in *My Grandfather's Son*.

Reverend Martin Luther King Jr. stands on the balcony of the Lorraine Motel in Memphis, Tennessee, on April 3, 1968, a day before he was assassinated in the same location. Accompanying him are (left to right) Hosea Williams, Jesse Jackson, and Ralph Abernathy.

Back in Savannah during Christmas vacation, he confided his disappointments in the Church and his doubts about becoming a priest to his parish priest and Aunt Tina. He returned to Immaculate Conception for another semester, still hoping to realize his grandfather's dream that he would become Savannah's first black priest.

Thomas's life changed on April 4, 1968, the day Reverend Martin Luther King Jr. was assassinated. When the news that he had been shot was announced, Thomas was following a white seminarian up the stairs. According to a *Newsweek* report, Thomas heard him say, "Good. I hope the [expletive] dies." At that moment, Thomas thought, "I knew I couldn't stay in this so-called Christian environment."

Thomas returned to his room and told his roommate, "I'm done here. I'm leaving. It's not a northern-southern thing. It's just a thing. It's no better here."

A few days later, he and a black friend drove to Kansas City to participate in a march in Dr. King's honor. Thomas recalled in his autobiography, "As I chanted and sang with the other marchers, I felt a fulfillment that I had never known at Conception Abbey . . . the seminary was surreal, far removed from the momentous turmoil in which America was now immersed."

Interestingly, biographers Merida and Fletcher quoted other students who remember the student body being just as upset at King's death as Thomas was. "The place was just in shock," recalled Frank Scanlon. "Maybe some idiot made that comment that Thomas remembers, but it sure didn't reflect the attitude of the people there."

Nevertheless, the other seminarian's insensitive words destroyed what Thomas and his grandfather had dreamed. "That was the end of seminary. That was the end of the vocation. That was the end of, for all practical purposes, my Catholic faith," Thomas told Steve Kroft on *60 Minutes*.

Myers Anderson was furious that Thomas was breaking his promise not to quit. As Thomas wrote in *My Grandfather's Son*, Anderson said, "You've let me down." Then Anderson went even further. "Because you're acting like a grown man and making decisions like a grown man, you have to live like one," Thomas remembered his grandfather saying. "No other man but me will live in this house. I want you to leave." Anderson refused to help Thomas further with his education. Thomas recalled Anderson saying, "You'll have to figure it out yourself. You'll probably end up like your no-good daddy or those other no-good Pin Point Negroes."

The relationship between Thomas and the man he had always called "Daddy" was never the same. Thomas moved in with his mother and worked that summer at the Union Camp bag factory in Savannah. With King's death and Robert F. Kennedy's assassination shortly after, Thomas was transformed.

"That summer I tore off the beliefs I had learned from Daddy and the nuns, the same way Clark Kent tore off his suit," he wrote in his autobiography. "The fog of confusion lifted. I knew what was wrong, who to blame for it, and what to do about it. I was an angry black man."

Tired of being one of the few black faces in all-white schools, he considered enrolling at Savannah State University, a small black college—but Sister Mary Carmine, one of his former teachers at St. John Vianney, had other ideas.

5

Wearing Combat Boots

Sister Mary Carmine was Clarence Thomas's high school chemistry teacher. When she heard that Thomas wanted to leave Immaculate Conception, she wrote to suggest that he try applying to the College of the Holy Cross, a Jesuit school in Massachusetts. On Thomas's behalf, Sister Mary Carmine asked a former student who was then attending the college to send an application to Thomas. Thomas did not want to go to a school in which only 25 black students had enrolled in 125 years. Out of respect for the nun, though, he applied, and he was accepted as a transferring sophomore. The $2,850 tuition was covered by a loan, a job, and a scholarship named after Martin Luther King Jr.

In September 1968, Thomas boarded the Silver Comet train from Atlanta and headed toward Worchester, Massachusetts. He had a $100 bill stashed in his shoe, a box of chicken on his lap, and a heart full of anger. "As the train pulled out of the

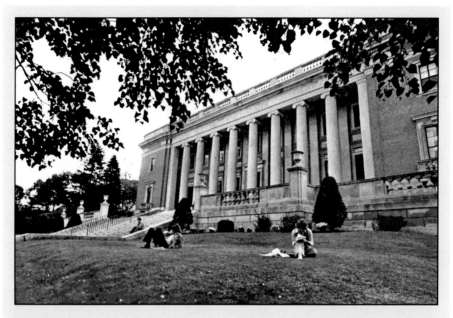

After leaving Immaculate Conception Seminary, Thomas attended the College of the Holy Cross in Worcester, Massachusetts. Above is a photograph of the college's Dinand Library, as it looked when Thomas was a student there.

station and Savannah vanished in the distance, so did the nice black boy from East Thirty-Second Street who had wanted nothing more than to be a priest," Thomas recalled in his autobiography.

When Thomas arrived at Holy Cross, he saw the white-trimmed, red brick buildings sitting high on a hill overlooking the town. Having become more progressive, the college's mandatory daily mass and a ban on alcohol had recently been dropped.

Thomas's day was broken into segments. He studied from 5:00 A.M. until breakfast. Then he attended classes for three to five hours. Track practice filled the afternoon. After that, he studied in the library until it closed at 7:00 P.M. Wedged in between all that, he worked in the college dining room, donning a white jacket to carry milk and plates of food to the tables. A quiet student, Thomas sat in the back of the classroom and rarely asked questions. He chose to major in English to continue to correct his Geechee dialect.

Holy Cross was perfect for Thomas's state of mind. As on other campuses throughout the nation, many students were outraged as the Vietnam War and racial injustice headlined the news. Thomas joined right in. He traded his religious uniform for a student radical's, wearing combat boots, army fatigues, and a black beret covered with "Black Power" buttons. In *My Grandfather's Son*, Thomas wrote, "I was furious with the Church, with Daddy, and with the condition of blacks in America, and now I was surrounded by other students who shared my fury."

In fall of 1968, Thomas helped organize the Black Student Union (BSU). The BSU campaigned for hiring black professors and administrators, sponsoring black studies and cultural events, and changing a phrase in the school's fight song from "old black Joe" to "go, Cross, go."

The BSU became a place for students to discuss politics and philosophy. Thomas loved the discussions and sometimes took an unpopular viewpoint just to stir things up. "He'd be the only person on one side, with 30 or 40 arguing against him," a classmate told *Newsweek*. "Half of the things he said I never believed."

Thomas did, however, oppose one of the BSU's proposals: the request for a dorm floor just for blacks. Thomas stated that he had come to college to learn to live with whites, not apart from them. He even proposed that, to promote integration, one black student should sit with white students at every meal, an idea that went nowhere. When the BSU voted, he was the only person in the 25-member group who voted against the segregated floor.

When the administration approved the all-black section, Thomas's friend, Robert DeShay, refused to move in. He had started to think that there was an expectation that all blacks had to think alike. "There became this pressure to conform to what the group had decided was appropriate behavior for black students on campus," he said in *Judging Thomas.* Years later, Thomas would observe the same thing. He would believe that the black community was trying to control his thinking and loudly protested against it.

Rather than give up his black friends in a protest against their self-created segregation, Thomas compromised. He moved into the black section, but he asked his white room-mate, John Siraco, to come with him.

HOLY CROSS PROTEST

Antiwar demonstrations occurred daily throughout the nation. During Thomas's junior year, in November 1969, more than 250,000 people marched in Washington, D.C., to protest. Holy Cross made headlines with its own campus upset.

On campus, another student group asked the BSU to help stop General Electric from conducting job interviews on campus. GE manufactured napalm, a jellied gasoline that was used in Vietnam to burn vegetation (and, not incidentally, civilians). On December 10, 60 or so members of the combined groups prevented about two dozen students from talking to the GE recruiters. Of the protesters, the school threatened to expel 12 white students and 4 black students. Blacks were outraged, as only one-tenth of the protesters were black but 25 percent of those charged with disruption were black. It looked suspiciously like racial discrimination. Meeting at the student-center office, angry BSU members talked of taking over a building by force and barricading themselves in it with chains and locks.

Thomas did not think that would work. He told Diane Brady in a 2007 *BusinessWeek* interview, "I said, 'Look, if we're not going to be treated fairly here, let's leave. And let's leave in a disciplined, professional way.'" Thomas believed that, by simply walking out, they would not break any rules, would support the expelled blacks, and would create a public relations nightmare for Holy Cross.

The BSU went along with Thomas's idea. When the administration announced that all 16 protestors were expelled, about 60 black students, dressed in suits and ties and carrying suitcases, gathered in a group, tore up their ID cards, and left the campus. After two days of bad publicity, school administrators backed down and granted amnesty to all of the students. "Nothing had happened to me personally," Thomas recalled of his part in the protest in Macht's biography, "but my friends were being treated unfairly. So I stood up for them."

Loyalty is one thing, but Thomas soon realized that he had flirted with a catastrophe of huge proportions. If he dropped out of school, even for the sake of his friends, telling his grandfather that he had left yet another school and thrown away a straight-A average would have been a complete disaster. Although he was not quite ready to end his career as a radical completely, he did back away from it.

In April 1970, Thomas attended an antiwar rally in Boston. "Once the organizers of the rally had gotten the crowd sufficiently worked up, they urged us to march to Harvard Square to protest the treatment of America's domestic political prisoners," Thomas wrote in his autobiography. "Off we went, chanting 'Ho, Ho, Ho Chi Minh' and demanding freedom for Angela Davis, Erica Huggins and anyone else we could think of." In addition to the frenzy of the rallying, the participants were drinking. The rally turned violent, and 3,000 protesters

IN HIS OWN WORDS...

In 2001, Thomas told a student audience, "One of my great regrets is that I knew so much when I was in college and was so angry and was such a Mr. Know-It-All that I missed so many opportunities to learn."

and 2,000 policemen tangled; nearly 200 people were injured. As stores were looted, police cars set afire, and windows broken, Thomas realized that he had forgotten why he was at Holy Cross in the first place: to get an education.

"I got back to campus at four in the morning, horrified by what I'd just done," he said in his autobiography. "I had let myself be swept up by an angry mob for no good reason other than that I, too, was angry. On my way to breakfast . . . I promised Almighty God that if He would purge my heart of anger, I would never hate again."

Thomas withdrew from group demonstrations and concentrated on his studies—and Kathy Ambush. A week after meeting her in February 1969, he told friends that he was in love. Thomas and Ambush dated for a year. Thomas played pool and darts with her father, went with the family on camping trips in New England, and joined them during holiday get-togethers. Her family was quite different from his own. While the Ambush family was close, Thomas and his grandfather were at odds, he saw his mother only occasionally, and his brother was far away in the Air Force.

Thomas was still a good student. He made the dean's list, was inducted as one of six (and the only black) into the Purple Key Society, and was named a Fenwick Scholar his junior year. During his senior year, Thomas decided to go into law, another field that his grandfather admired. He wanted to go back to Savannah "to begin helping some people," he told Holy Cross's news service.

On June 4, 1971, Clarence Thomas graduated from Holy Cross with a 3.5 grade point average (B+). His grades had earned him acceptances from law schools at Yale, Harvard, and the University of Pennsylvania. The day after graduation, he and Kathy Ambush were married at All Saints Episcopal Church in Worcester, Massachusetts. His mother and grandmother attended his graduation and the wedding. Aunt Tina baked and sold pies to pay for her trip there. Myers Anderson, the grandfather who had played such an important role in Thomas's life, sent word that someone had to stay behind to tend the farm animals, so he could not attend. "Whatever the reason, his refusal was a cruel and hurtful blow," Thomas wrote, "and it deepened the chasm that now separated us."

YALE LAW SCHOOL

With a college degree and a new wife, Clarence headed to Yale Law School in New Haven, Connecticut. By the fall of 1971, Thomas was one of 12 blacks in Yale's 165-person freshman class. The school had an affirmative-action plan, which made being a member of a minority group as important a qualification for admittance as good grades. The plan caused some minority students to wonder if they got into the university

Earl Warren (Chief Justice 1953–1969)

Earl Warren (1891–1974) was born in Los Angeles and attended the University of California, Berkeley, both as an undergraduate and as a law student. He served three terms as governor of California (1942–1953) and resigned early from the third when newly elected president Dwight D. Eisenhower appointed him chief justice of the Supreme Court.

Chief Justice Warren and his Court championed civil rights and civil liberties. During his 16 years as chief justice, the Court's rulings on segregation, school prayer, school busing, the death penalty, and criminal rights changed the face of American law. It was in front of the Warren Court that Thurgood Marshall argued the 1954 case *Brown v. Board of Education*, which established that "separate but equal" was unconstitutional, boosting the then-fledgling civil rights movement. The Court's decision in *Miranda v. Arizona* made the Miranda warnings ("You have a right to remain silent; you have the right to an attorney. . . . ") a part of our society. Prior to 1964, the size of voting districts varied so much that, in California, one state representative represented 6 million people in Los Angeles County whereas another one represented 14,000 in a rural county. Warren's Court forced the states to redraw their districts so that one man's vote would be worth the same as another's in the legislature.

because they were good enough or because they were black. Furthermore, Yale believed that its students were the best in the country, so the law school did not give letter grades or rank their students, which otherwise could have been a measure by which to prove that black students did well.

About the system, Thomas said, "You had to prove yourself every day because the presumption was that you were dumb and didn't deserve to be there on merit," according to the book *Supreme Discomfort*. "Every time you walked into a law class at Yale, it was like having a monkey jump down on your back from the gothic arches."

Thomas avoided classes that he thought a black might be expected to take. He concentrated instead on traditional business, tax, and property law. He took more than the maximum

Critics called the Warren Court a "super-legislature" because its rulings (not the Congress) made these changes. President Eisenhower, who had intended to appoint a conservative justice, was surprised. "The biggest damned-fool mistake I ever made," he later said about nominating Warren.

Warren, the crusader for individual rights, was not so generous after the Japanese attack on Pearl Harbor. As governor of California, he supported Japanese internment camps, telling Congress, "The only reason that there has been no sabotage or espionage on the part of Japanese-Americans is that they are waiting for the right moment to strike." An executive order, signed by President Roosevelt, put 120,000 Japanese Americans (two-thirds of whom were American citizens) in concentration camps that were scattered from California to Arkansas. Later, Warren wrote, "I have since deeply regretted the removal order and my own testimony advocating it, because it was not in keeping with our American concept of freedom and the rights of citizens. Whenever I thought of the innocent little children who were torn from home, school friends and congenial surroundings, I was conscience-stricken."

Warren resigned from the Court in 1969 and was replaced as chief justice by Warren Burger. Warren continued to be active in speaking and writing until his death in 1974.

class load and signed up for the most difficult courses. Once, he got a poor grade from one of Yale's toughest teachers. Rather than avoid the teacher, he decided to sign up for other courses with that professor and wrote his senior term paper under his tutelage. He earned the highest grade possible for it. Years later, he was angered by any suggestion that he was accepted at Yale because of affirmative action.

Thomas and his wife lived off campus, but he spent most of his time at school. Most people work 40 hours per week; Thomas studied 50 hours and then worked 15 more hours at a part-time job. He arrived at school to study by 6:00 A.M., ate breakfast at 7:00 A.M., went to classes, and then studied in the library. On the days he worked at his part-time job, he did not get home until midnight.

At Yale, Thomas no longer wore his battle fatigues; instead he dressed in bib overalls or work pants with suspenders. He topped off his outfit with a denim hat. "He dressed like a Georgia farm boy," one of his professors told the authors *of Supreme Discomfort.* "He looked like he came right out of a cornfield."

Thomas had both white and black friends at Yale, although he acted differently with each group. To his white friends, he was shy and reserved. With his black friends, he was outgoing and known for his loud belly laugh and his jokes. "Clarence was an incredibly funny guy, very witty," said classmate Dan Johnson. "He had a bag of jokes you wouldn't believe. . . . He kept me in stitches."

No one knew until years later that Thomas felt that the white professors at Yale treated their white and black students differently. No one knew that he felt uncomfortable at the university. "It wasn't about them," he told *BusinessWeek*'s senior editor, Diane Brady. "I just didn't fit. I don't fit in an orchestra. I don't care how great the orchestra is. It's nothing against Yale. . . ."

On February 15, 1973, Thomas's wife gave birth to a boy they named Jamal Adeen. With a family to support, money was another concern for Thomas. During his first summer in law school, he worked at New Haven Legal Assistance Association, a group that provides legal assistance to low-income or otherwise disadvantaged clients. Thomas was so well liked that the agency offered him a job—twice—but he refused. He wanted to return to Savannah. The next summer, Thomas got a job at a prominent black law firm in Savannah, where he was paid $100 per week. Thomas and his family stayed at his grandparents' house in town while Anderson and Aunt Tina stayed on the farm. The Thomases spent their money carefully, keeping track of their grocery purchases to stay within their budget.

During his last year at Yale, Thomas concentrated on landing a high-paying job for after graduation. Recruiters from large law firms buzzed around the university, hoping to hire top students. When they interviewed Thomas, they assumed that he would want to do civil rights work with poor people instead of corporate law. Thomas was irate. According to *Supreme Discomfort*, he said, "I went to law school to be a lawyer, not a social worker. If I want to be a social worker, I'll do it on my own time."

He interviewed with several firms in Atlanta. One seemed about to hire him as its first black associate, but with Yale's system (no grades, no class rank), Thomas could not demonstrate how well he had done in school. The firm hesitated.

Then Thomas met John C. Danforth, Missouri's attorney general. The young Republican promised that Thomas would not work on civil rights cases. Danforth promised to treat him like anyone else and work him harder for less money than any other job in America. His offer, less than $11,000 per year, was peanuts compared to Thomas's classmates' future salaries. "Some of my classmates warned that I had wasted a Yale law degree," Thomas later said in *Supreme Discomfort*. "Others laughed, and some seemed to look at me with pity."

With a backlog of 5,000 cases to process, Danforth joked about the position. "There's plenty of room at the top," he promised. Mark Tushnet later wrote that Thomas responded,

When John C. Danforth offered Thomas a job at the Missouri attorney general's office, he promised to work Thomas hard and not to stick him with the civil rights cases. Danforth would eventually leave the attorney general's office to become Missouri's representative to the U.S. Senate. He is shown here in 2005.

"Easy for him to say. He was white. I was black." Nonetheless, Thomas accepted the position.

Later, the Atlanta firm that had hesitated did offer Thomas a job, but, having given his word to Danforth, he could not accept. Ken Foskett recorded in *Judging Thomas* that Thomas's application to the firm was filed away with a note: "A real overachiever. Predict he will do well wherever he decides to go."

Clarence Thomas graduated from Yale on May 20, 1974. His wife, her parents, and a cousin were in the audience. Once again, Myers Anderson was not there to see his grandson's success.

6

Skin Deep

Clarence Thomas has never been able to shed his skin. From his Yale admittance to his Supreme Court nomination, one of Thomas's chief assets has been his color. Even his first job, working for John Danforth, began as race related. After being elected Missouri's attorney general, John Danforth came to Yale in 1973 to staff his office. "I was looking for a black lawyer," Danforth admitted in *Judging Thomas.* "Politically, I thought that was important." He achieved that goal by hiring Thomas.

Thomas could not begin his job—and get paid—until he passed the Missouri Bar exam. Studying in St. Louis during the summer, Thomas was so broke that he tried unsuccessfully to sell his blood at a local blood bank. Three days after passing the exam in September 1974, he went to work, arguing his first case before the Missouri Supreme Court in Jefferson City. "My legs were rubbery and my stomach queasy as I climbed the stairs to the Supreme Court," Thomas wrote in his autobiography. "For a moment I wanted to run away." He did not run. He presented his case and sat down. His law career had begun.

Danforth treated everyone on his staff of 30 equally. Thomas was assigned an overwhelming caseload, just like everyone else. He worked first on criminal appeals and then in the revenue-and-taxation division. In his best known case, he argued that the state could eliminate "vanity" plates, something that influential people fought against. He won. "Nobody ever supervised me," Thomas recalled. "I was my own man. It wasn't black this and black that. I didn't have to play any roles. . . . You got to be you."

Being Clarence Thomas meant shooting hoops in the gym and shooting the breeze about politics with colleagues. "He was the type who'd go into a room without knowing anyone," *Newsweek* reporter Michael Boicourt said. "Before he left, he'd have talked to everyone, and they'd all like him."

Thomas's take-home pay was $560 a month, about $10 less than his bills required. Thomas and his wife washed their clothes by hand and hung them in the backyard to save money. Years later, according to *Judging Thomas*, Thomas would say of his job with Danforth, "It was the best job I ever had."

In 1976, Danforth was elected to the U.S. Senate and Thomas went to work as an attorney for the Monsanto Chemical Company in St. Louis. There, Thomas was remembered as a sharp lawyer and a likeable person. "He was one of those guys who kept you laughing a lot," said a co-worker, who recalled a time for *Supreme Discomfort* when Thomas was asked to lower his voice in the hall. He responded by stooping low to the floor and kept on talking.

Thomas's autobiography told a more sobering story. Despite the fact that his salary at Monsanto was twice what Danforth had paid, Thomas was not content. His assignments at Monsanto, focusing on the disposal of toxic waste and agricultural products, were not challenging enough. His marriage was troubled, and he took comfort in drinking.

In 1979, John Danforth, by then the Republican senator from Missouri, asked Thomas to come to Washington, D.C., as a legislative assistant. Thomas jumped at the chance to work for his old boss. Again avoiding racial issues, Thomas specialized in energy and environmental cases.

A year later, Thomas crossed the boundary into a political no-man's-land for blacks. He registered as a Republican, a step that started him toward the Supreme Court. He explained in *My Grandfather's Son*, "I saw no good coming from an ever-larger government that meddled . . . in the lives of its citizens, and I was particularly distressed by the Democratic Party's ceaseless promises to legislate the problems of blacks out of existence."

Shortly afterward, at a conference in San Francisco, Thomas talked to Juan Williams, a *Washington Post* reporter. He explained his developing opposition to integration, affirmative action programs, and busing. He wanted blacks to depend only on themselves, not on government help, to succeed. Williams's story on December 16, 1980, featured Thomas's conservative ideas. Thomas was quickly criticized for not "thinking black." In a speech years later, he said, "I was shocked at the public reaction. I had never been called such names in my entire life."

Shortly after Christmas, Thomas's marriage cracked. He moved in with a friend and slept on the living room floor. He later wrote in his autobiography that money was sometimes so short he had to choose between a Burger King meal and transportation. "If I ate, I walked; if I rode the bus, I went hungry," he recalled.

Even as he struggled, the Reagan administration had noticed this conservative black Republican. In spring 1981, he was offered a job as the assistant secretary for civil rights in the Department of Education. Thomas did not want to take the position—he thought that his color had inspired the offers. "What other reason besides the fact that I was black?" he asked, according to *Supreme Discomfort*. His friends urged him to reconsider, however, and he did take the job. This led to a February 1982 offer—which he also thought was motivated by his race—to become chairman of the Equal Employment Opportunity Commission (EEOC). Once again, he reluctantly took the position. At age 33, Thomas took charge of an EEOC that could not pay its bills and sometimes sent checks to people who had died. Unresolved cases were stacked to the ceiling. The Republicans opposed government regulation of business and hated the EEOC. The Democrats and civil rights leaders hated the Republicans who ran it. Nevertheless, the EEOC's job was to enforce the Civil Rights Act of 1964, a set of laws that barred racial, religious, age, or gender discrimination. With 3,200 employees and a budget of $141 million, it had to be fixed.

Thomas took charge of an agency he called "the dungeon." Over time, Thomas upgraded its computer recordkeeping and the agency righted itself financially. Officially, as its chairman, Thomas was tough and unyielding. He once informed an employee that she was fired by taping a note to her chair. Unofficially, he inspired great loyalty. He often visited with employees, inquiring about their families and asking for their suggestions before changing policy.

Thomas drew critics from the start. He did not like to use statistics to decide if discrimination had taken place, and he did not like the use of quotas to remedy discrimination if it had. He did not agree, for example, that employers had to make their workforce 30 percent black just because the community's population was 30 percent black. He did not agree that promising to hire more minorities in the future corrected past discrimination against individuals.

Civil rights leaders were angered that he opposed these types of affirmative action. "You were helped by it," they told him. "You wouldn't be where you are if not for it."

Chairman of the EEOC Clarence Thomas speaks at a press conference after a settlement between General Motors, the EEOC, and the United Auto Workers in 1983.

Thomas felt, though, that there was too much of a risk that real achievements by blacks could mistakenly be credited to preferential treatment through affirmative action rather than the hard work of the individuals themselves. For example, he remembered the doubts that potential employers expressed over not knowing his grades at Yale. Civil rights organizations also accused Thomas of forgetting who he was and where he came from because he did not accept their views. Thomas later defended himself in his 2007 autobiography: "That kind of all-us-black-folks-think-alike nonsense wasn't part of my upbringing, and I saw it as nothing more than another way to herd blacks into a political camp."

During Thomas's first two years at the EEOC, he experienced several family crises. On March 30, 1983, Myers Anderson collapsed at his kitchen table in Savannah. He died shortly after. Thomas was crushed. The last time the two had spoken, they had patched up their relationship and embraced for the only time in their lives. Thomas had looked forward to happier times with his grandfather. "We agreed that the reason the two of us always had such a hard time getting along was because we were so much alike," Thomas recalled in his autobiography. At the funeral, Thomas wept uncontrollably.

Tragedy continued. A month later, on May 1, his grandmother, Tina Anderson, suffered a stroke and passed away. Then, in 1984, after 13 years of marriage, Thomas's divorce from Kathy Ambush was finalized. Thomas took custody of 11-year-old Jamal, whom he called "the Mighty Dude."

Thomas was consumed by grief and by the worries of paying his rent and credit card bills. Thomas later recalled in *My Grandfather's Son* that he told his secretary, "If I so much as tripped and fell I didn't think I had it in me to stand up again."

A NEW LIFE

Despite his EEOC controversies, Thomas was nominated for a second term as chairman in 1986. He was also named one of Washington's most eligible bachelors by *Jet* magazine.

At a civil rights forum in New York in May 1986, Thomas met Virginia Lamp, a 30-year-old labor relations attorney. Lamp, a native of Omaha, Nebraska, had been interested in Republican politics since high school and dreamed of running for Congress. She worked in Washington, D.C., for the U.S. Chamber of Commerce. At first, Thomas and Lamp decided to be "just friends." Both were dating other people, and Thomas was not interested in a new serious relationship, much less one with a white woman. "I had more than enough problems without adding that one to the list," he wrote in his autobiography. Lamp liked his hearty laugh, though, and their common interests drew them together across the color line. Thomas told his friends, "I know what it's like to be unhappy," *Newsweek* reported. "This is someone I'm happy with."

As their relationship developed, Lamp wrote a letter to her parents to head off objections they might have to her relationship. She told them that, if they could not accept the man who made her happy, then they would lose their daughter. "But he was so nice, we forgot he was black," said Lamp's aunt according to *Supreme Discomfort*, "and he treated her so well." On May 30, 1987, Lamp and Thomas were married in a Methodist church in Omaha. Jamal was Thomas's best man. The Thomases bought a home in a new development in Alexandria, Virginia, just outside Washington, D.C., and lived a quiet suburban life that included planting flowers, lawn mowing, car washing, and attending neighborhood barbecues.

Living with Virginia and Jamal and enjoying his son's participation in sports, Thomas relaxed. Of his fortieth birthday he wrote, "I'd never been happier. At long last, I had found peace."

In the meantime, however, controversy was roiling in Washington. President Reagan had nominated Robert Bork, a conservative legal scholar, to the Supreme Court. Liberals opposed Bork, who believed in a strict, narrow interpretation of the Constitution called "originalism." They feared that he would overrule civil rights and social justice laws that blacks, women, and others had achieved through a broad reading of the Constitution.

Forty-five minutes after Bork's name was first announced for the seat, the battle lines became clear. Liberal senator Edward Kennedy said, "Robert Bork's America is a land in which women would be forced into back-alley abortions, blacks would sit at segregated lunch counters, [and] rogue police could break down citizens' doors in midnight raids." The political atmosphere went downhill from there.

Thomas supported Bork, however, and was disgusted by the way he was treated. Little did Thomas know that the Bork fight would be a picnic compared to what lay ahead for him. The Senate rejected Bork, and he returned to the U.S. Court of Appeals. He resigned shortly afterward.

With President Reagan's term ending, Thomas faced the end of his EEOC job. He might have gone into the business world if George H.W. Bush, who became president, had not asked him to take Judge Bork's seat on Washington's U.S. Court of Appeals. This was no small proposition. Many believed that the appeals court was a training camp for future Supreme Court justices. In fact, Supreme Court justice Thurgood Marshall, who was black, was getting ready to retire from the Court. Getting experience as a judge positioned Thomas perfectly for Marshall's seat. "I think everybody recognized it would be next to impossible to name a nominee to that seat who wasn't black," one official said, according to Merida and Fletcher in *Supreme Discomfort*.

Thomas was not much interested in being a judge. The job did not pay all that much, and Thomas, only 41 years old, wanted a black Corvette. "I'm not serious enough," he said to an aide. Once again, though, his friends persuaded Thomas to accept. EEOC staff members were sorry to see him leave, and

Sandra Day O'Connor (Associate Justice 1981–2006)

Sandra Day O'Connor once said that being chosen as a justice "is probably a classic example of being the right person in the right spot at the right time. Stated simply, you must be lucky."

Sandra Day was born March 26, 1930, on an Arizona cattle ranch 25 miles (40 kilometers) from the nearest neighbor. She could drive by age seven, shoot a rifle, and ride a horse by age eight. She was also a bright student and attended Stanford University, where she overlapped her senior year as an undergraduate with her first year at the law school. She was in the same class as William Rehnquist, who was appointed to the Supreme Court in 1971. (He took the seat of chief justice in 1986.) Rehnquist graduated first in the class, and O'Connor was third. In 1952, she married John Jay O'Connor, another law school student. Although Stanford Law School is one of the best schools in the nation, because of O'Connor's gender, only one law firm would hire her on graduation—and not as a lawyer, but as a legal secretary.

Later, O'Connor started her own small law firm, raised three boys, and served as assistant state attorney general. She persuaded the Arizona governor to appoint her to fill a state senator's seat, and she was elected to to honor his efforts at the agency, the EEOC dedicated its new office building to him.

FEDERAL COURT OF APPEALS

In July, the Senate voted 98 to 2 to confirm Clarence Thomas as a judge on the D.C. Court of Appeals. "I was surprised to find that I liked the job," he later wrote. It was quite a change. He had a staff of five instead of hundreds, he could determine his own hours, and he got along well with the other judges.

Thomas was one of 12 judges on the Court of Appeals. While at the court, he liked to sit in his chambers, smoking huge cigars and thinking about abstract law. In total, Thomas wrote 19 opinions while on the bench, although none revealed how he would interpret the Constitution. His salary increased to $133,000, and he finally bought the black Corvette. Then,

the Arizona State Senate twice more. One of her first bills was a repeal of a discriminatory 1913 law that prevented women from working more than eight hours a day. In 1973, she became the first female majority leader in any state. She later was elected to a state judgeship.

During his campaign for the 1980 presidential election, Ronald Reagan promised to appoint the first woman to the Court. He was elected, and, when Justice Potter Stewart announced his retirement in 1981, Reagan nominated O'Connor because of her conservative views about the Court's role in government. She told the Senate Judiciary Committee, "I do not believe it is the function of the judiciary to step in and change the law because the times have changed. I do well understand the difference between legislating and judging." The Senate confirmed her by a vote of 99–0.

Her votes surprised court observers. The conservatives thought that she would vote conservatively—particularly on abortion—but she proved to be the Court's "swing vote" during the 25 years she served. With the rest of the Court's justices voting predictably either conservatively or liberally, O'Connor's vote often decided the outcome of a ruling. Justice O'Connor retired in 2006 to care for her husband, who has Alzheimer's disease.

Thurgood Marshall, the first black Supreme Court justice, was appointed by President Lyndon B. Johnson in 1967. He is pictured here outside of the Court building shortly after he was sworn in.

15 months later, his life changed. On June 27, 1991, Justice Thurgood Marshall, 83 years old and until then the only black Supreme Court justice, announced his retirement.

President Bush invited Thomas to Kennebunkport, Maine, his vacation residence. Thomas thought that he was going for an interview, but he suspected that more was coming when the

First Lady congratulated him. "I guess I let the cat out of the bag," Thomas recalled her saying. The president and Thomas talked in the president's bedroom. The president wanted to know if Thomas could "call them as you see them" and if he could survive the confirmation process.

"I've been confirmed four times in the past 10 years," Thomas told the president. "I think we can manage once more." Bush then told Thomas that he was about to announce Thomas as the nominee to replace Marshall. "I about died," Thomas said, according to Macht's biography. "It had gone from interviewing to being the nominee in about 20 minutes, and I am sitting there wondering, 'What happens next?'" At 2:00 P.M. that day, the president and Thomas faced the press. Thomas wrote in his autobiography, "The press corps gasped. 'It's Thomas,' someone blurted out."

President Bush said, "I believe he'll be a great justice. He is the best person for this position. . . . He's excelled in everything he has attempted." Political experts nearly choked. Thomas had been a judge for a little over a year. He had never argued a case before a federal appeals court, much less the Supreme Court. He had not written one scholarly article that revealed his philosophy. It was obvious to everyone what his primary credential was: his skin color.

Thomas stood behind the podium and thanked those who had helped him: his grandparents, the nuns at his high school, and his family. He told the press, "Only in America could this have been possible." He said that he looked forward to the confirmation process and to serving his country and "to [being] an example to those who are where I was and to show them that, indeed, there is hope."

Hope would be the last thing his confirmation process would show. Even during the president's announcement, most believed that he would be confirmed. No one imagined that Clarence Thomas would shortly find himself nearly devoured by controversy.

7

Piranhas Feeding

The July 1, 1991, news of Clarence Thomas's Supreme Court nomination sent people scrambling. The Bork hearings had created an all-time low in the search for information against any Supreme Court nominee. Reporters used the same tactics for Thomas. They snooped in his garage and rummaged through his garbage, seeking clues to what he ate, what kind of cigars he smoked, what he read, and even what he doodled on scraps of paper. They looked into the church he attended and interviewed employees at the EEOC. They traveled to Pin Point and Savannah, photographing and interviewing his family. The search for damaging information resembled a feeding frenzy. *Newsweek* reported that journalist Juan Williams was contacted by Senate staff members who asked, "Anything on your [interview] tapes we can use to stop Thomas?"

Thomas's life had been prodded and poked during four confirmation hearings. There should have been no surprises.

The White House had quizzed him about intimate details of his divorce and remarriage before announcing his nomination. Nothing ever surfaced.

Thomas and the conservative ideas he represented, however, became a target for abortion-rights groups, civil rights organizations, and labor unions. They scoured his hundred speeches and 30,000 documents, looking for ammunition that could keep him from getting on the Court and possibly voting against the causes that they held dear.

Chief among his opponents were those who supported abortion. Pro-choice groups feared that, with Thomas providing a fifth vote, the conservative Supreme Court justices who were against a woman's right to choose would overturn *Roe v. Wade*. They did not want that abortion law thrown out.

Many black leaders were also against him. They could not support a black man who loudly and frequently criticized affirmative action, welfare, and school busing—all policies that they believed helped African Americans come closer to racial equality. "I don't see how we can support someone who stands against everything we stand for," said one board member of the National Association of the Advancement of Colored People (NAACP). Thomas met with NAACP leaders and impressed them with his "blackness" and his loyalty to his "roots," but still the NAACP board, the Congressional Black Caucus, the Leadership Conference on Civil Rights, and the nation's largest black church group, the National Baptist Convention, decided to oppose him.

One strategy that his opponents used was to attack Thomas personally. Their insults were intended to build public opinion against him. *USA Today* columnist Barbara Reynolds charged, "If he can't paint himself white he is going to think white and marry a white woman." *Judging Thomas* reported that 75-year-old black feminist Flo Kennedy said, "I'm embarrassed as a black person that they ever found this little creep. Where did he come from? We're going to Bork him. We need to kill him politically."

Virginia Thomas, wife of Clarence Thomas, listens to Thomas's opening statement during his confirmation hearings before the U.S. Senate Judiciary Committee.

Rumors surfaced that, because Thomas had praised Louis Farrakhan's ideas of self-help for blacks, he also shared Farrakhan's hatred of Jews. Rumors circulated that he had beaten his first wife. More rumors said that the Thomases attended a church that worshipped snakes. Stories sprang up that Thomas had watched pornographic movies in college.

Another strategy was to attack Thomas's qualifications. His critics pointed to his short term as an appeals judge and his lack of written opinions, conveniently forgetting that several other Supreme Court justices had been confirmed without being judges. They also brought up that he had never practiced law except in Missouri.

Thomas saw the criticism for what it was. He wrote in *My Grandfather's Son*, "What that *really* meant, of course, was that I dared to hold views of which my opponents disapproved. . . . I had to be stopped, whatever the cost."

Conservatives across the country agreed with Thomas's assessment. They also remembered the bloodletting of Robert Bork's nomination. They were determined that that would not happen again.

GETTING READY

Thomas prepared for three long, grueling months. First, he and his advisors filled 70 pages answering the Judiciary Committee's questionnaire. Thomas studied thick notebooks filled with important cases and articles on the death penalty, school prayer, and affirmative action. The right to privacy, which included positions on abortion, filled two entire notebooks.

Every day, Thomas started studying at 4:00 P.M. He no longer mowed the lawn, went to the movies, attended church, or

IN HIS OWN WORDS...

In *My Grandfather's Son*, Thomas wrote:

By summer's end my critics seemed like the low-country gnats that infested our Liberty County farm. I remembered how they'd swarmed at me from every direction as I walked through the fields in the cool hours before dawn. This wasn't so different—except that these gnats were lethal.

drove his car. Instead, he met with advisers to discuss what he had read during the morning or the night before. He studied Judge Bork's disastrous hearings and the videotapes of David Souter, whose noncontroversial testimony succeeded where Bork's had failed. His advisers formed a "murder board" that peppered him with hostile questions he might be asked. They advised him on how to act, what to say, and how to avoid controversy during the weeks before the September hearings. It was not an easy job to pull off. One of his advisors, Mike Luttig, recalled in John Danforth's *Resurrection* that Thomas was "very headstrong," that "he had his own views," and "nobody tells Clarence anything."

"I felt as though I was entering the second stage of a triathlon, staggering out of the water and climbing onto my bicycle for a hundred-mile ride, knowing that I still had to run a marathon after that," Thomas wrote in his autobiography.

Thomas understood that he had to play politics to get the confirmation. One long-established tradition that he followed was visiting senators' offices to let them become acquainted with him informally. It was an opportunity for them to see beyond his conservative ideas to the likable and outgoing man his friends knew. Most nominees only visited key players, but Thomas called on 59 of the 100 senators.

THE HEARING

The hearing before the Judiciary Committee began on September 10, 1991. Thomas knew that he faced intense questioning. Walking down the halls to the Caucus Room with his wife, Thomas recalled in *My Grandfather's Son*, "My stomach heaved, and my legs felt like they were carved out of wood."

The 14 members of the Judiciary Committee spread out in a line behind a massive desk. Thomas sat behind a small desk in front of them. Dressed in a dark suit and red tie, the 43-year-old Thomas sat nervously adjusting his glasses and folding and

Clarence Thomas raises his right hand as he is sworn in for his confirmation hearings. When questioned during the hearings, Thomas responded with vague answers about his conservative positions, infuriating some members of the Senate Judiciary Committee.

unfolding his arms in front of him. Behind him sat his wife, his son (now 18 years old), his mother, and his sister.

Senator Joseph Biden, the committee chairman, swore Thomas in, and then each senator spoke. Some obviously supported him; others outlined their opposition.

It was 3:00 P.M. before Thomas's turn came. As his advisers had told him, he began with the "Pin Point strategy." He described the poverty of his early life, the instances of prejudice and discrimination he had experienced, his rescue by his grandparents and nuns, and the successes hard work had brought him.

Then, for five days, Thomas played verbal dodgeball with the committee. He responded to its questions about his conservative ideas with vague and general answers. Having seen Justice Souter easily survive his confirmation hearings, he softened his answers, seeming to agree and then disagree with opinions he had once publicly spoken. He seemed to forget what he had said in the past. "He had been totally coached out of saying anything he thought," said a supporter quoted in *Judging Thomas.*

That infuriated the Judiciary Committee and everyone listening. According to Senator Paul Simon in *Advice & Consent,* Senator Howard Metzenbaum said on the second day of the hearings, "We don't know if the Judge Thomas who has been speaking and writing throughout his adult life is the same man up for confirmation before us today."

Senator Biden thought so as well. According to transcripts published on the Web site of the First Amendment Center, Biden told Thomas, "They now talk about the Souter standard, how Souter didn't answer questions that some suggest he should or shouldn't have . . . we're going to have a new standard, the Thomas standard, which is you're answering even less than Souter."

Thomas later admitted that he was not being himself. "You have to play sort of rope-a-dope," he said in *Resurrection.* "You have to lay back and you have to take more than you normally would take. . . . And by playing by those rules, the country had never seen the real person."

Roe v. Wade was the hot button issue in the hearings. Thomas's responses were maddening to both the pro-lifers and pro-choicers. Senators asked and re-asked, more than 70 times, for his opinion on a woman's private right to choose to have an abortion. Thomas's answer did not vary. He repeated, "Do I have this day an opinion, a personal opinion on the outcome of *Roe v. Wade*; and my answer to you is that I do not."

Martin Garbus, a legal expert, believes that Thomas may have had opinions about it on other days, but the important phrase in Thomas's answer was "this day." Garbus believed that Thomas did not have an opinion about it on that particular day in September. Thomas would not even admit to having discussed *Roe v. Wade* during his years studying law, an answer that left listeners dumbfounded. They could not believe that a law student would not have discussed the most controversial

Louis Brandeis (Associate Justice 1916–1939)

When Clarence Thomas was appointed to the Supreme Court, his critics did not think he had enough experience as a judge—as if being a judge were a requirement to be a justice. In fact, less than half of the justices to date were judges before they became justices.

One Supreme Court justice who had not been a judge before his Court appointment was Louis Brandeis. He was called "the people's attorney" because he often helped ordinary people and common workers in cases that involved minimum wage or safe working conditions. He created the "Brandeis Brief," which lawyers now almost always use to argue their cases. It included descriptions, facts, and studies of how ruling one way or another could affect society.

Brandeis's opponents, who often lost to him, were big business corporations such as insurance companies and railroads. These were powerful enemies who fought hard to keep him off the Court. Former President William Howard Taft and former presidents of the American Bar Association challenged his "fitness" to be on the Supreme Court. His confirmation battle lasted six months, twice as long as Thomas's, and longer than that of any other justice in Supreme Court history.

Once on the Supreme Court, Brandeis became one of the Court's most outstanding justices. He championed individual rights, such as free speech and privacy, over those of big business and big government. In *Olmstead v. United States*, in which a man was convicted on the basis of wiretaps, Brandeis wrote that people have a right to be left alone and that privacy is one of our most precious rights. He also believed that the legislatures, not judges, should make law.

Brandeis was the first Jewish Supreme Court justice. Because of that, a fellow justice, James Clark McReynolds, refused to sit next to him and left the room whenever Brandeis spoke. Brandeis served for nearly 23 years and was replaced by William O. Douglas.

opinion that the Supreme Court handed down in the past half century. In his 2007 autobiography, Thomas explained, "The fact was that I'd never been especially interested in the subject of abortion, and hadn't even read the decision until it turned up in one of Mike's many binders."

Thomas testified for 25 hours in total. Some of the questioning was so heated that, according to Macht's biography, Thomas's sister, Emma Mae, said, "If I wasn't a Christian I'd take my Bible and slap that senator in the head." Thomas's mother was equally angry with the Democrats' rough handling of her son. He recalls she told him, "I ain't never votin' fo' another Democrat long as I can draw breath. I'd vote for a *dog* first."

Thomas finished testifying on September 16. Then, 90 witnesses testified both for and against him. Among them were his eighth grade teacher, Sister Virgilius, and the dean of Yale Law School, who recalled Thomas as a hard-working and diligent student. Black witnesses split. Some praised his independent thinking. Others criticized him sharply for his scorn of affirmative action, a policy that had helped thousands of blacks, including Thomas himself.

Rosa Parks, whose refusal to move to the back of a Birmingham bus in 1955 had sparked the civil rights movement, watched the proceedings from the audience. She told Senator Paul Simon, "With what he stands for, he shouldn't be permitted to use Martin Luther King's name."

When the hearings concluded, most agreed that Thomas had won no fans on the Judiciary Committee during the process, but he had not said or done anything that would cost him his confirmation. The Judiciary Committee voted on September 27, splitting 7 to 7. Under Senate rules, the tie sent the nomination to a full Senate vote where most thought he would be confirmed. Unknown to Thomas, disaster lurked just around the corner.

8

The Scandal

"Anita? You can't—you've got to be kidding," Thomas said. "This can't be true."

Before the Judiciary Committee hearings began, rumors surfaced that Thomas had sexually harassed Anita Hill, who had worked at the EEOC when he was chairman. These rumors reached the staffs of Thomas's opponents, Senators Howard Metzenbaum and Edward Kennedy. Behind the scenes, staffers contacted her. From September 9 to September 21, Anita Hill discussed her charges on the condition that Thomas would not be told her name. There was even talk, Foskett reported in *Judging Thomas*, that she would testify from behind a screen, an idea that Senator Biden vetoed. "That's ridiculous," he said. "This isn't the Soviet Union."

By September 23, Hill agreed to talk to the FBI and to allow Thomas to be informed that she was his accuser. Two days later, two FBI agents relayed her charges to Thomas and interviewed him. He was flabbergasted. He could not believe that she would do such a thing and angrily denied the charges.

The FBI's investigation uncovered no evidence to support Hill's story. The Senate majority and minority leaders were told about Hill, and some of the Judiciary Committee saw Hill's four-page statement. No one suggested a private meeting with Hill or a postponement of the vote. After the Judiciary Committee's 7 to 7 split, the full Senate scheduled debate for October 3 and its vote October 8.

A staff member of the Judiciary Committee leaked Hill's charges to the media, however. On October 6, a New York newspaper printed her story, and National Public Radio interviewed Hill about the charges. It became a nationwide scandal. Thomas's support in the Senate evaporated. His mentor, Senator Danforth, asked for a delay of the vote until what Thomas later called "the scum story" could be investigated.

Thomas was shattered and humiliated by Hill's charges. "I feel like someone has reached up inside me and ripped out my insides," Thomas said, according to *Supreme Discomfort*.

Thomas's friends wondered where the sexual harassment occurred. According to Thomas, he had hired Hill 10 years before at the Department of Education. When he moved to the EEOC, she wanted to follow him there. "You're a rising star," he remembered her saying in his autobiography, "I want to go with you."

Later, he helped her get a teaching position at Oral Roberts University in Oklahoma. Telephone records revealed that Hill had called Thomas a dozen times over the years. Still, Hill charged that Thomas had pressured her to date him, and that, when they talked privately, he turned the conversation to sex.

Macht's biography described a former EEOC associate's saying, "Thomas had put Hill's name on the list of people he wanted to testify for him. . . .Would he have listed her to speak for him if there had been anything that smacked of sexual harassment?"

According to Thomas's autobiography, he hardly recognized the Hill who stepped into the media spotlight: "She had transformed into a conservative, devoutly religious Reagan-administration employee. In fact, she was a left-winger who'd never expressed any religious sentiments whatsoever during the time I'd known her."

Thomas was so upset that his friends hardly recognized him either. The humorous, outspoken, confident Clarence Thomas disappeared and was replaced by a man who could not eat or sleep. The new Thomas, according to *Judging Thomas*, paced about wild-eyed, hyperventilating, bursting into tears, and muttering, "This was a friend. This was someone I tried to help."

On October 11, 1991, the Judiciary Committee reconvened the hearings. Thomas would speak first and then Hill would be questioned. For Thomas, that day would become the most important in his life. His reputation and his future hung on his statement.

When he sat down to write that statement the night before, Thomas was mentally and physically exhausted. His first draft was garbled and too short. When they read it, his advisers panicked. In *Resurrection*, Thomas is quoted telling his wife, at 11:30 P.M., "I'm tired, I'm exhausted, I'm scared."

Up again at midnight, he sat down at the kitchen table and tried to write again. Having returned to his faith during the hearings, Thomas told Danforth that he said, "Let me open up to the Holy Spirit. Then I just started from square one. Not with other people's ideas. I looked at the draft and I just started writing. I continued writing."

He wrote on a legal pad until 5:00 A.M., while Virginia retyped his statement on the computer. Thomas recalled lying down to rest until 6:00 A.M., but he did not sleep. "I spent the hour tossing, turning and thinking, and the more I thought the angrier I got," he said in his autobiography.

Getting angry was an important step. Clarence Thomas the fighter was back. On Friday morning, October 11, Thomas returned to the Russell Senate Building. According to Danforth, while en route to the Caucus Room, Thomas told an adviser, "I'm going to be okay. I'm going to let them have it."

With his wife and Danforth sitting behind him, Thomas began quietly, apologizing for anything he might have said or done that offended Anita Hill. Then, the anxious, uncertain nominee who had dodged the Committee's questions about the Constitution completely disappeared. The real Clarence Thomas took charge.

William O. Douglas (Associate Justice 1939–1975)

Once confirmed, a justice serves on the Supreme Court until he retires or is impeached for reasons of "judicial misconduct." William O. Douglas's opinions and lifestyle provided plenty of ammunition for possible impeachment proceedings.

In 1951, Douglas caused a stir by suggesting that the United States recognize China in order to drive a wedge between the two powerful Communist countries, the Soviet Union and China. Communist China was hated by politicians and ordinary Americans alike. Some members of the Senate thought that Douglas should be impeached for making such statements.

Two years later, Julius and Ethel Rosenberg, convicted of treason for selling atomic secrets to the Soviets, were sentenced to death. Their attorneys brought the case to Douglas and explained that a technicality in the law might show that they were illegitimately sentenced to death. Douglas issued a temporary stay of execution. On hearing about it, the chief justice reconvened the Court for an emergency session to overturn the stay. Afterward, Douglas's enemies implied that he had Communist ties, and they attempted to initiate impeachment proceedings. In 1966, Douglas shocked Washington by marrying for a fourth time. He had divorced his first wife to pursue Mercedes Davidson, a married woman. He was married to her until he met Joan Martin. Once, he hid Martin, his future third wife, in his office closet

He went on in a booming voice, "Enough is enough. I am not going to allow myself to be further humiliated in order to be confirmed. . . . No job is worth what I have been through." To those who did not know Thomas, it appeared that he was about to withdraw his name from confirmation. Clarence Thomas the competitor, however, would not do such a thing. Instead, he told them, "My name has been harmed. My friends have been harmed. There is nothing this committee, this body, or this country can do to give me back my good name. Nothing."

Despite his advisers' suggestions that he remain in the Caucus Room when Hill testified, Thomas left and returned home. He did not even watch her on television. Instead, he smoked

to prevent Davidson from discovering her. He divorced Martin and married Cathleen Hefferman, a college student whom he met while she was working as a waitress in a cocktail lounge. "Wild Bill's" love life caused several senators to call for impeachment proceedings on moral grounds.

In 1969, the Nixon administration opened hearings to impeach Douglas as revenge for the Democratic Congress's rejection of the Republican administration's nominee for the Supreme Court. Republican Gerald Ford, then the House minority leader, strung together a group of facts that implied that Douglas supported pornography, advocated the overthrow of the government, and had gambling and mob connections. To support his ex-wives, Douglas had written books and articles to supplement his income; one of his articles appeared in *Playboy* and an editor who had served time for distributing pornographic material bought another article about folk singing. Portions of one of Douglas's books were reprinted in a magazine interspersed with pictures of naked women. Douglas also took money from an organization thought to have gambling and mob connections.

Ford's accusations inspired 110 congressmen to call for an investigation of "judicial misconduct." After 10 weeks, the investigation found no direct evidence that Douglas had done anything improper. Douglas stayed on the Court until 1975. His 36 years was the longest tenure that any justice served.

Before Thomas's confirmation hearings began in September 1991, rumors surfaced that a former employee of his was accusing Thomas of sexual harassment. A month later, Anita Hill testified about her claims to Senate Judiciary Committee (shown above).

a cigar and listened to music while Virginia watched the hearings in another room.

Anita Hill testified about repeated suggestive remarks that she said Thomas had made to her and spoke of the X-rated films he had described. She described the stress and anxiety she had felt while working with him. She spoke calmly, confidently, and convincingly for eight hours. The committee grilled her on her story, but she did not change it. *Time* magazine reported that she said, "I am not given to fantasy. This is not something I would have come forward with if I was not absolutely sure of what I was saying."

As Hill ended her testimony, Danforth recommended that Thomas reappear before the Committee and the television cameras to keep Hill's testimony from becoming the only thing the news played that night. Thomas returned to Danforth's office and lay down before his 8:00 P.M. reappearance.

"Jack," he remembers saying, "This is a high-tech lynching."

"If that's what you think," Danforth recalls he said in *Resurrection*, "then go upstairs and say it."

Thomas returned to the Caucus Room. He heatedly denied that he had ever tried to date Hill. He heatedly denied that he had ever had any sexual interest in her. He heatedly denied harassing her. Then he took on the United States Senate Judiciary Committee. "I think that this hearing should never occur in America," he told the men in front of him. "This is a case in which this sleaze, this dirt, was searched for by staffers of members of this committee, was then leaked to the media, and this committee and this body validated it and displayed in prime time over our entire nation," he said, according to *Supreme Discomfort*.

Thomas was furious. He nearly trembled with anger. He glared at the committee members, and then he spoke the most shocking and memorable words of his career. They would be quoted again and again for decades. "This is a circus," he said, according to CNN tapes. "It's a national disgrace." Thomas sat back in his chair for a moment and then leaned close to the microphone.

> And from my standpoint as a black American, as far as I'm concerned, it is a high-tech lynching for uppity blacks that in any way deign to think for themselves, to do for themselves, to have different ideas, and it is a message that unless you kowtow to the old order, this is what will happen to you. You will be lynched, destroyed, caricatured by a committee of the United States Senate rather than hung from a tree.

Thomas leaned back again, clenched his fists, and stared at each committee member. Virginia took her eyes from her husband and looked at the committee as if to say, "What do you think about that?"

The committee was speechless. Thomas had reminded whites of the shameful acts of the past and reminded blacks how painful these events had been. Senator Biden looked up and down the table, hung his head, and then called on another senator to take over. Thomas answered questions for another 90 minutes. He firmly denied each of Hill's allegations. "I am incapable of proving the negative," he told Senator Howell Heflin. "It did not occur." He jabbed his finger in the air. He told them, "You have spent the entire day destroying what it's taken me 43 years to build."

Back in Danforth's office, Thomas was told that the White House phone lines had jammed with callers, most of them supportive of Thomas. "The American people are in an uproar!" Danforth told Thomas in *Resurrection.*

In the Caucus Room, former employees of Thomas testified to his integrity in dealing with women. A second woman's statement that Thomas had sexually harassed her was entered into the record but not discussed. The Judiciary Committee voted down a motion to extend the hearings 12 to 2. They simply did not have the will to draw out the dirty political soap opera any longer. The slimy episode ended at 2:03 A.M. on October 14.

Later, people had differing views of Thomas's lynching remarks and the race card he had thrown in the face of the committee. Some agreed with him. "I felt that he really was being lynched," said his friend Cliff Faddis in Macht's biography, "just like in the old days, with a rope and no justification. I was not surprised when he put it that way. That was pure Clarence Thomas."

Others were angry that Thomas, who had spent all his life asking that his race be ignored, referred to it in such shocking terms. "He's trying to get the issue off of him, and get in on racism," a black woman told the *New York Times.* "He's an angry man."

Three days of hearings solved nothing. Hill's version and Thomas's version of their relationship never matched. She believed that he had harassed her; he said that he had never asked her out. He said that she had wanted to follow him to the EEOC; she said that she went because she was afraid she that could not find another job. He said that she called him many times after she left his employ, congratulating him on his marriage and asking for advice. She called the phone logs "garbage."

Both Hill and Thomas were intelligent and articulate. Both spoke clearly and with passion. The *New York Times* quoted a medical student saying, "Each person sounds so believable. How do human beings judge?"

Millions thought that Clarence Thomas had lied under oath—an impeachable offense for a judge. "I'd say Judge Thomas has a problem because of the graphic detail she is providing," a Chicagoan said to the *New York Times*. Other millions believed that Anita Hill had lied under oath. "Why wouldn't she have said it at the time," another *Times* article reported. "It's hard for me to believe something that happened years ago is just coming out now. Maybe she is just seeking publicity."

It was a toss-up in the news magazines as well. *Time* reported that, when Thomas was at Holy Cross, he wrote a poem that urged black men to respect their women. *Newsweek* quoted Hill's fellow law professor saying, "Every faculty member here believes in Anita's integrity and honesty."

The situation was both disgusting and sad. A resident in Anita Hill's hometown said, "It's not about justice. It's about which side is going to win. This wasn't about Anita Hill or Clarence Thomas. It was just politics, dirty politics at that."

Even Senator Joseph Biden agreed that nobody won. "The judge was wronged. Anita Hill was wronged. The process was wronged," he later said.

On the last day of the hearings, Hill's lawyer announced that Hill had taken—and passed—a polygraph test. Thomas's people countered with a quote from Senator Kennedy: "If you

This picture was taken outside of Thomas's home, just after Thomas was confirmed as a Supreme Court justice. Of his bitter confirmation battle, Thomas said, "We have to put these things behind us. We have to go forward."

are an altar boy, you probably will fail [a polygraph]. But who passes it? The psychopaths, the deceptive ones." Some wanted Thomas to take a polygraph test, too, but he refused.

On Tuesday, October 15, the full Senate debated the merits of Clarence Thomas's confirmation. Clarence and Virginia

Thomas remained at home during the debate. Thomas was in the bathtub when the voting began. His wife asked if he wanted to watch the vote. "Absolutely not," Thomas replied, "I don't care what they do. God never got me into anything that He didn't get me out of." A few minutes later, his wife told him that the Senate had voted 52–48 to confirm him. The process had taken 107 days.

"Whoop-de-damn-do," Thomas said, and he stayed in the hot water.

Later that evening, close friends celebrated at the Thomas house. News media crowded outside, waiting for Thomas's reaction. Given the high emotions of the event, his security detail insisted that he wear a bulletproof vest to meet with reporters. Standing in the rain, he recorded in *My Grandfather's Son,* "I think that no matter how difficult or how painful the process has been, that this is more a time for healing, not a time for anger or animosity. . . . We have to put those things behind us.

9

Riding the Magic Carpet

"It was like we were riding this magic carpet," said Virginia Thomas after the Senate vote put her husband on the Supreme Court.

On October 18, 1991, Clarence Thomas was sworn in on the White House's South Lawn. Thomas's son, mother, sister, brother, and other family members sat with about 1,000 guests. Advisers, politicians, and friends, including Sylvester Stallone and baseball great Reggie Jackson, looked on. Senator Danforth delivered the opening prayer.

Although Thomas would not officially become a justice until he took the judicial oath, the Republicans wanted to celebrate his victory over his opponents. The Marine band played from the Truman Balcony, while television stations provided live coverage of the event.

"Clarence Thomas has endured America at its worst, and he's answered with America at its best," President Bush said,

Clarence Thomas takes the Constitutional oath to become an associate justice of the U.S. Supreme Court on October 18, 1991. Behind him stand President George H.W. Bush and Thomas's wife.

according to the *New York Times*. "He brings that hard-won experience to the High Court and America will be the better for it."

When it was his turn to speak, Thomas spoke about both the past and the present. "There have been many difficult days as we all went through the confirmation battle, and I mean we all," Thomas said in the same *New York Times* article. "But on this sunny day in October, at the White house, there is joy. Joy in the morning."

Five days later, on October 23, Thomas's wife, Senator Danforth, and an administrative assistant watched Clarence Thomas become the one-hundred-sixth justice of the Supreme Court. Chief Justice Rehnquist administered the official judicial oath, and Thomas promised to "administer justice without respect to persons, and do equal right to the poor and to the rich."

Of course, Thomas did not forget his confirmation ordeal. He continued to question Anita Hill's motives and remained furious at the media and liberals who opposed him. He rarely appeared in public or made speeches, he quit reading newspapers, and he became quieter.

"An experience like that leaves scars," said a friend in a 1992 *Time* magazine article. "Clarence and his wife have both had to go through a healing process."

THE WORKPLACE

The place where Clarence Thomas works, and most likely will work for the rest of his career, is a majestic structure made of brilliant white marble. The architect purposefully designed 44 steps in front of the building so visitors have to climb *up* to the highest court in the land. The roof rests on 16 marble Corinthian columns 92 feet above everything. Normal talking dials down into whispers when visitors pass the massive statues and six-and-a-half-ton bronze doors into the building.

From the first Monday in October until June, the justices work quietly in their offices. Behind heavy oak doors, Thomas's chambers are decorated with portraits of Booker T. Washington and Frederick Douglass and a bronze bust of his grandfather, Myers Anderson. He also displays the statue of St. Jude, the patron saint of hopeless causes, that a white seminary student once broke. "That's what they called me," he said in *Supreme Discomfort*, "a hopeless cause."

The justices must determine which hundred or so cases out of 6,000 to 9,000 requests include some constitutional issue that they must decide. They carefully study cases and research laws that relate to the chosen cases before hearing the oral arguments in the Supreme Court Courtroom.

The courtroom resembles a Roman temple, with marble walls and two dozen marble columns that stretch 44 feet high. Floor-to-ceiling windows are draped with burgundy velvet curtains. The justices sit in black leather chairs at a raised mahogany desk. Decorations include pewter drinking cups, a spittoon that is used as a wastebasket, and white quill pens like those used by our country's forefathers. Attorneys sit at tables in front of the justices. Each lawyer has 30 minutes to explain his or her side of the case. The justices often interrupt to ask questions.

After the oral arguments, the justices convene in a private conference room. Before getting down to discussion, they shake hands, a symbolic gesture that reminds them that they are working together. In order of seniority, each justice explains his or her thinking on the case. Then they vote. The chief justice assigns two justices to write opinions—one to explain the majority vote (the way the case is decided) and one to explain the minority vote (the way those who disagreed wanted the case to go). Justices can change their votes any time before the decision is announced. Rough drafts of the opinions circulate among the justices until the final version is settled. Each justice can write his or her thoughts in an individual opinion as well. The rulings are made public near the end of the term, sometime in late spring or early summer.

The process must proceed on schedule. There can be no thought of "I think I'll do this later." David O'Brien recounted in *Storm Center* that Thomas called his first 5 years his "rookie year" and has said, "In your first 5 years, you wonder how you got here. After that you wonder how your colleagues got here."

ROOKIE RULINGS

From day one, Thomas was expected to jump right in to the routine—without any instructions or orientation. The Court's term had already begun, and a thousand pages of legal documents in metal carts awaited his review.

Although he was emotionally and physically exhausted from his confirmation battle, Thomas worked hard. He got up at 4:00 A.M. and was settled at the Court building by 5:30. He worked 12-hour days, with breaks in the gym for shooting baskets and working out. He took work home with him and studied over the weekends.

Within two weeks of his swearing in, Thomas had donned his judicial robes, zipped up his conservative views, and voted on cases. When the Court's rulings were announced, Thomas's philosophy became clear. Thomas is conservative, an "originalist," a "strict constructionist," and favors "judicial restraint."

He told a group of Hillsdale College seniors in 2007, "I like to go back to the Constitution, looking at the history and tradition along the way." Thomas interprets the Constitution narrowly, measuring a case against the "original intent" of the Founding Fathers. He studies what words meant during colonial times and looks at other laws during that time. If the Constitution does not mention a particular issue, originalists want the Court to use "judicial restraint" and to stay away

IN HIS OWN WORDS...

In *My Grandfather's Son*, Thomas wrote:

The black people I knew came from different places and backgrounds—social, economic, even ethnic—yet the color of our skin was somehow supposed to make us identical in spite of our differences. I didn't buy it. Of course we had all experienced racism in one way or another, but did that mean we had to think alike?

from making new laws. They want state governments or Congress to step in.

Thomas is not a judicial activist. He does not believe in a "living Constitution," and he does not "read into" its words something that can apply to modern society. In 1973, judicial activists legalized abortion in *Roe v. Wade*. They based their ruling on "a woman's right to privacy." That phrase is not mentioned anywhere in the Constitution. They "read it into" the Constitution (in fact, the document does not specifically refer to a "right to privacy" for anyone). Critics believe that the Supreme Court wrote that law (which is Congress's job) and based it on the justices' personal beliefs (not the Constitution). Many laws that women's groups and civil rights groups treasure came out of decisions from activist Courts.

As his views became known, Thomas's votes on the Court were loudly criticized. By the end of his first term, his public image was badly scorched. It began with Keith Hudson, a prisoner serving 20 years in a Louisiana penitentiary. In 1983, Hudson was washing his clothes in his toilet when a guard told him to stop flushing it. According to Merida and Fletcher, Hudson responded, "I'm washing my clothes. I live here. You just work here."

Two guards shackled, handcuffed, and then beat Hudson. The beating caused him to urinate blood, loosened his teeth, and cracked a dental plate. Surprisingly, nothing required medical attention. Hudson claimed that his Eighth Amendment rights against "cruel and unusual punishment" had been violated. The case made its way through the court system up to the Supreme Court.

The Court took the case to decide if force against a prisoner that caused "only" minor injuries could be called "cruel and unusual punishment." In February 1992, the Court ruled that it did. Thomas was one of two who did not agree. As an originalist, Thomas believed that the Eighth Amendment's "cruel and unusual punishment" phrase originally applied only to prison *sentences*, not to the prisoner's *treatment* in prison. According to Foskett's biography, Thomas wrote, "Abusive behavior by prison guards is deplorable conduct that properly evokes outrage and contempt. But that does not mean that it is invariably unconstitutional."

Court watchers were shocked that Thomas, who had experienced poverty and discrimination, voted against Hudson. A *New York Times* editorial called him, "the youngest, cruelest judge," describing his opinion as "alarming" and "a crashing disappointment" to people "sure he would bring to the Court the understanding bred of hardship."

William Howard Taft (Chief Justice 1921–1930)

William Howard Taft never dreamed of becoming president. That was his wife's ambition for him. What he really wanted to be was chief justice of the Supreme Court. Taft was the only man to serve both as president and chief justice of the Supreme Court; thus, he was the only man to head both the Executive Branch and the Judicial Branch of the federal government.

Taft was born on September 15, 1857, to a politically active family in Cincinnati, Ohio. Taft attended Yale College and then returned home to earn his law degree at the University of Cincinnati Law School. Taft practiced law in the city for several years, until he was appointed as a state judge in 1887.

Taft's association with the federal government began when President Benjamin Harrison named him the U.S. solicitor general in 1890. After a successful stint as the first civil governor of the Philippine Islands (then a territory of the United States), Taft returned to Washington, D.C., as a member of then-president Theodore Roosevelt's cabinet. Taft's role with Roosevelt's popular administration ensured that he would be easily elected. He served as the twenty-seventh president, from 1909 to 1913. During his term, New Mexico and Arizona were admitted as states, and Congress passed and ratified the Sixteenth Amendment, which made a federal income tax possible. Taft had trouble with Progressives, however, who thought that he was not pursuing his predecessor's agenda with enough enthusiasm, and he lost his bid for reelection. Later, he wrote, "I don't remember that I ever was president."

As president, Taft appointed six justices to the Court (more than any other president except George Washington, who appointed the first Court,

A columnist wrote to Thomas, "I don't expect that you will always do what strikes the rest of us as 'the right thing.' But why go out of your way to do the wrong?" The Hudson case established Thomas's reputation as harsh and hard hearted despite his other, less controversial votes.

As Jeffrey Toobin wrote in *The Nine,* "There were two kinds of cases before the Supreme Court. There were abortion cases—and there were all the others." Just six months after Thomas was confirmed, "the case" arrived on his desk.

Abortion was the real reason that Thomas's confirmation hearings had been so vicious. During the hearings, pro-choice

and Franklin Roosevelt, who appointed eight justices). Some believe that Taft's hope to become chief justice was the reason he appointed 65-year-old, overweight Edward D. White to the seat in 1910. White held his position for a few more years, though, and Taft had to wait until 1921. Only then did President Warren Harding appoint him to the Court. As chief justice, Taft oversaw a reorganization of the federal court system that allowed the Supreme Court to take on only cases of national importance and to work more efficiently.

For the first 146 years of its existence, the Supreme Court had had no permanent place to operate. It met in a private home, a tavern, city hall, and rooms in the Capitol building, where Congress is housed. For a country that prided itself on "separation of powers," having the Supreme Court camp out in the Capitol building seemed a bit shabby. Because they had no offices, the justices had to do most their work at home. Taft had lobbied for a building for the Supreme Court since 1912, the last year of his presidency. In 1929, Chief Justice Taft convinced Congress to build a permanent building. It pledged $9,740,000. The project came in under budget, and $94,000 was returned to the United States Treasury.

Taft never saw the magnificent marble building completed. He died in 1930, 2 years before construction began and 5 years before it was completed. He was, however, immortalized above the west entrance. One of the statues above the columns portrays him as a young man. Busts of all the chief justices, including Taft, line the Great Hall that leads to the courtroom.

supporters, who believe that a woman has a right to choose to terminate a pregnancy, attacked Thomas because they thought he would vote to overturn *Roe v. Wade.* Pro-lifers supported Thomas just as strongly—for the same reason.

In April 1992, *Planned Parenthood of Southeastern Pennsylvania v. Casey* arrived at the Supreme Court. Although abortion was legal in Pennsylvania, the state's laws made it difficult for women to legally get one. It required them to wait 24 hours, forced them into counseling on abortion alternatives, and obliged married women to inform their husbands. It also required minors to have permission from a parent. The Court was supposed to rule on these restrictions. Anti-abortion activists, however, wanted the Court to decide if *Roe v. Wade* itself was constitutional.

Although eight justices were appointed by Republican presidents (who are generally against abortion), the Court did not do what the anti-abortion crusaders wanted. It ruled 5-4 that almost all of the restrictions could stand—but it did not make abortion illegal.

Thomas voted in the minority. He signed Chief Justice Rehnquist's and Justice Scalia's dissenting opinions, which said that the abortion issue should be left up to the states to decide and that "*Roe* should undoubtedly be overruled." At last, everyone knew where Thomas stood on abortion. Pro-lifers loved him; pro-choice supporters hated him even more.

Because Thomas and Justice Scalia often vote the same way, Thomas's critics have concluded that Thomas is "a Scalia puppet," unable to think for himself because he is not as intelligent as the white justice. The pairing of himself and Thomas irritates Justice Scalia. *Supreme Discomfort* quotes Scalia: "It's a slur on me as much as it is a slur on him—like I'm leading him by the nose. I don't huddle with Clarence and say, 'Clarence, this is what we're going to do.' Really, it ticks me off."

Many liberals and civil rights leaders expected the black justice to vote "black," championing a case because it benefitted—or came from—his own race. Thomas's rookie cases showed that they were often going to be disappointed. Although Justice Thurgood Marshall had lobbied to write "color" into laws to help disadvantaged blacks, Thomas wants no part in favoring any minority.

For example, Thomas watchers thought that he would interpret the law broadly in a case that involved Lawrence C. Presley, the first black commissioner in Etowah County, Alabama. Four white commissioners stripped Presley of his authority to manage the road construction money in his district. The Court, including Thomas, voted that Presley's rights had not been violated under the 1965 Voting Rights Act. They ruled that the act applied only to voters, not to elected officials. Presley was stunned by Thomas's vote. *Time*'s online magazine reported that Presley said, "Black people here learned a lesson from this. Just because he's black does not necessarily mean that he's positive."

In 1994, Thomas would not support the creation of specially designed black voting districts. By redrawing districts, more black officials could have been elected. In *Holder v. Hall*, he wrote that minorities do not always think alike and that he did not want people grouped together by race.

A 1995 case that involved affirmative action once again showed that Thomas believes that minorities should not receive special treatment. The Court upheld affirmative action, but Thomas dissented, calling for a ban on it all together. He wrote that singling out a race to *help* it was just as bad as singling it out to *oppress* it. "These programs," he wrote, "stamp minorities with a badge of inferiority and may cause them . . . to adopt an attitude that they are entitled to preferences perhaps indefinitely."

Because of these views, many in the black community regard him as a traitor to his race. Black magazines have portrayed him as an "Uncle Tom," an "Aunt Jemima," or a Judas. Justice Scalia cannot understand the black community's scorn. "There are more Italian Americans who are liberal than conservative," he told *Supreme Discomfort's* biographers, "but they're all proud of me."

In 2007, Thomas told a group of students from Hillsdale College, "I never set out to be unpopular, but popularity isn't of high value to me. I set out to do my best to be right. I am who I am." Those who watch the Court, and Clarence Thomas, have come to realize just that.

10

The Last Laugh

Over the years, two Clarence Thomases have walked toward the spotlight. One is the Justice Thomas who inspires strong reactions by Court watchers. Those who hold his views adore him. Those who do not agree with his philosophy strongly denounce him. Once, in 1998, Thomas addressed the National Bar Association, an organization of black lawyers that is critical of his decisions. He told the audience of 2,000 that he had come "to assert my right to think for myself, to refuse to have my ideas assigned to me. . . . I come to state that I'm a man, free to think for myself and do as I please. But even more than that, I have come to say that isn't it time to move on? Isn't it time to realize that being angry with me solves no problems?" The group remained unconvinced.

Away from the Supreme Court and the headlines that it inspires, there is another Clarence Thomas. This Clarence Thomas is relaxed and easygoing. He enjoys Louis L'Amour western novels, gardening, and traveling around the country in a 40-foot motor home. He is usually well-liked by those who hear his hearty laugh.

This Clarence Thomas adores his grandnephew. Marky Martin came into his life in 1997. Marky's father, Mark Martin (Thomas's nephew), was in prison; his white mother was a Head Start teacher, struggling to raise three children. Drawn to the 6-year-old, Clarence and Virginia volunteered to adopt Marky and give him a stable home—much like Thomas himself had found in his grandfather's home. "It seemed like it turned back the clock 10 years on his life," said a former clerk in *Supreme Discomfort.*

Thomas, then 49, returned to the role of parent, adjusting his Court work schedule to pick up Marky at school, play football and basketball with the boy, and fuss over his difficulties with reading and math homework. Marky adjusted well to the Washington, D.C., environment. Thomas talks about Marky

DID YOU KNOW?

Judges first began to wear black robes in 1694 as a symbol of mourning for the death of England's Queen Mary. Many of England's colonies copied the custom.

The first chief justice of the Supreme Court, John Jay, decked himself out in a flowing black, red, and silver robe. Justices of the Supreme Court began to wear black robes at the suggestion of John Marshall, the fourth chief justice of the United States. The idea was to make the men fade into the background so that the law could be more important. Marshall also convinced the justices to live together in a boardinghouse so that they could discuss cases over dinner and Marshall's excellent wine. He persuaded them to vote as a group rather than to have each write his own opinion of the case, though this custom did not last long.

In the twentieth century, Chief Justice William Rehnquist (1986–2005) added three gold stripes to each of his sleeves, copying a costume he saw in an opera. His successor, John Roberts, did not continue the custom and returned to the all-black robe.

Thomas spoke to the National Bar Association in July 1998. He is shown here signing autographs after his speech. The NBA, an association of black lawyers, was founded in 1925 at a time when blacks were not welcome in the American Bar Association.

with the other justices and in his speeches. *Supreme Discomfort* said that Thomas's favorite Marky story concerns the boy's ideas about his biracial heritage. When asked his race, Marky replied that he was Italian.

In November 1999, Thomas fulfilled a longtime dream to own a motor home. Since then, the 40-foot vehicle—complete with leather furniture and satellite television—has taken Thomas, his wife, and Marky away from Washington politics. On the road, Thomas hangs around in jeans, parks in Wal-Mart lots for the night, and makes pleasant conversation with other RVers. Picking up a Spirit of America Award in 2004, he told an audience of 200 RV executives that he had seen much of the United States from behind the wheel. "RVing allows me to get out and see the real America. In RV campgrounds, you wave at everybody and they wave back. . . . We're all here for the same reason."

Some of the other justices love opera and playing bridge and golf, but Thomas prefers the pastimes he has enjoyed throughout his life. A knee injury sidelined his basketball and football workouts, but he is a devoted Dallas Cowboys and Nebraska Cornhuskers fan. He loves NASCAR racing. Decked out in a black-and-orange leather jacket with "Daytona 500" on the sleeve, Thomas served as the honorary grand marshal of the 1999 race. His job that day, like Alabama governor George Wallace before him and President George W. Bush after him, was to say, "Gentlemen, start your engines."

Thomas fills up a room with his sense of humor. He is well liked by his fellow justices, as well as cafeteria workers and security guards. "A most congenial colleague," said Justice Ruth Bader Ginsburg in *Supreme Discomfort.*

He regards his clerks as "family," loaning his car or offering a spare bedroom when they are in need. He has invited them to his home and hosts reunions of former clerks. Ken Foskett's *Judging Thomas* told of a time when he noticed that a clerk's tires were thin. He took time to show the clerk how to measure tire wear and told her about a tire sale.

For years, Thomas's critics have observed his silences during oral arguments. Other justices interrupt lawyers to ask questions; Thomas does everything but. He looks at the ceiling, covers his eyes with his hands, and whispers or writes notes to the justice next to him. One reason that Thomas's critics give for his closed mouth is that he is not smart enough to ask intelligent questions. Others, like renowned trial lawyer Martin Garbus, believe that his mind is made up on a case before the oral arguments. Garbus said, "He could mail in his decisions for the year at the beginning of the term."

Yet another theory offered by Supreme Court observer Jeffrey Toobin (author of *The Nine*) is that, because so much has been made about his silences, Thomas "wasn't going to give his critics the satisfaction of seeing him change his ways." Thomas will talk openly with young people, however. In a 1999 speech, he said the favorite part of his job was "talking to the youth, it doesn't matter what walk of life, what color, age. . . . It really is inspiring."

His comments to one boy in a school tour of the Supreme Court provided one answer. When the boy asked why he did not speak during oral arguments, Thomas replied, "I had grown up speaking a kind of dialect. It's called Geechee . . . people praise it now. But they used to make fun of us back then. . . . When I transferred to an all-white school at your age, I was self-conscious. I was thinking in standard English but speaking another language. . . . I just started developing the habit of listening."

On another occasion, Thomas urged a group of Virginia fifth graders who were visiting the Court to work on homework instead of watching television. One boy asked if Thomas ever did something that was not good for him. Thomas admitted that he smoked cigars. Thomas then promised the

IN HIS OWN WORDS...

In his book *Judging Thomas: The Life and Times of Clarence Thomas*, Ken Foskett quotes Thomas on the judicial system:

> I have been frustrated from time to time. I have gone back to my chambers and just thrown up my hands—"What are these people thinking?" But I will still say, in all that frustration, that we are the envy of the world, and for good reason. We don't have revolutions when we change our governments. We don't have wars when we have differences of opinions. We have a system to solve our disputes, to resolve our disputes. And it works.

student, "I will never smoke another cigar if you promise me that for one year you will do your homework instead of watch television." *Supreme Discomfort* reported that he walked back to his office and threw away the expensive cigars he loved to smoke. The next year, he saw the student again. "Well guess what?" Thomas told the boy. "I haven't smoked a cigar." However good his intentions, though, Thomas could not stay smoke free. He did return to the cigars. As a government official confessed, they are "Good cigars, real good cigars. And I get sick every time I smoke one with him."

Conclusions that Thomas ignores his race are disproven by his actions. Thomas actively helps many African Americans. In his biography of Thomas, Ken Foskett told of Thomas's efforts to help a disadvantaged but gifted student get into a private school. Thomas found someone who was willing to pay for the boy's tuition from fifth through twelfth grades.

Thomas often works quietly behind the scenes to help out. Though he could speak at large universities and address important people elsewhere, in 1998, he appeared at a "graduation" for drug addicts. As an observer said, "One of the nine most powerful people in the world [is] out at a youth home speaking to a bunch of former drug addicts and gang members."

During the confirmation hearings, Thomas returned to his faith, reading the Bible and praying with partners. Since then, he has attended an Episcopal church in Washington frequently. In interviews, he credits getting through the confirmation controversy to prayer; he seldom comments more, saying that that part of his life is private.

Thomas's philosophy has not changed much since 1991. After a vote in 2007 that ruled that integration plans in Seattle and Louisville were unconstitutional, the *New York Times* compared Thomas's opinions in 1991 and 2007. "We don't get smarter just because we sit next to white people in class," he said in 1991. In 2007, he said, "In reality, it is far from apparent . . . that integration is necessary to black achievement."

Yet, people still blink twice. Conservatives love him; others do not.

Depending on who is talking about Thomas, he has been called the Court's "most fascinating justice" and "the most radical justice." He remains opposed to affirmative action, believing that blacks can be successful through hard work and self-reliance rather than through government assistance. He believes that the Declaration of Independence protects individuals rather than group rights. He believes that any law can be overturned—no matter how long it has been in force—if it doesn't line up with what the Framers of the Constitution intended.

The basis of the 2007 case *Morse v. Frederick* was a student who had displayed a banner that said "Bong Hits 4 Jesus" across the street from the school at a school-supervised event. The principal suspended the student, who then sued the school, eventually taking the case to the Supreme Court. Thomas agreed with the Court that the principal had not violated the student's freedom of speech. He went even further, though, saying, "In light of the history of American public education, it cannot seriously be suggested that the First Amendment 'freedom of speech' encompasses a student's right to speak in public schools."

By far, the biggest splash in 2007 was the publication of Thomas's autobiography. The normally media-shy justice seemed to be everywhere as he promoted the book in several magazines, on a four-city book tour, on CBS's *60 Minutes,* on Fox's *Hannity & Colmes,* and on the radio show of his friend Rush Limbaugh.

The book, *My Grandfather's Son*, had been in the works since Thomas received a $1.5 million advance for the manuscript—an amount no other justice has received for his or her memoirs. He explained to Sean Hannity that his brother and mother helped him name his autobiography. "They always said, you're just like your grandfather. We called him

Clarence Thomas laughs during a presentation at Marshall University in West Virginia. On the left is Brent Benjamin, a justice of the West Virginia Supreme Court.

'Daddy' . . . and when I thought about it after I had written much of the book, I said, 'Well, I am my grandfather's son.'"

He has said that he wrote the book to show that he experienced some of the same problems kids have today and hopes to provide kids with "some of the guidance that could help them with their lives." The autobiography also provided him a chance to give his version of the events in his life. It pays tribute to his grandfather and retells his up-from-the-bottom rise from poverty. It describes other, lesser-known parts of his life, such as a past cycle of heavy drinking and struggles with debt. It also reveals that Thomas is still an angry man. He still blames the searing confirmation hearings he had to endure on those out to squelch his independent thinking. He is still angry with the media.

Opinions of the book's value vary depending on how readers view Thomas. A *New York Times* editorial shortly after the book came out said, "The rage he harbors raises questions about whether he can sit as an impartial judge in many of the cases the Supreme Court hears."

A book review in the conservative magazine *Human Events* said that calling him angry "is an attempt to cheapen the value of the message and the . . . numerous messages of hope, faith, and beauty that are the soul of *My Grandfather's Son*."

During the interview that was part of the book tour, conservative talk show host Sean Hannity told Thomas, "This is an extraordinarily honest book."

Not surprisingly, Anita Hill, now a professor at Brandeis University, did not like the book's descriptions of her. In an Op-Ed piece in the *New York Times,* she said, "I will not stand by silently and allow him, in his anger, to reinvent me." She said that others had come forward after the hearings to support her accusations. She pointed out that she did not have "mediocre" qualifications, as Thomas had charged, but rather graduated from Yale, like Thomas, and passed the tough District of Columbia bar exam. She called his description of her religious convictions "nasty." "I stand by my testimony," she said.

During Thomas's time on the bench, the Court has changed. Stephen Breyer joined the court in 1994. Conservative chief justice William Rehnquist died and was replaced by another conservative, John Roberts, in 2005. Justice Sandra Day O'Connor, the influential "swing vote," retired in 2006 and was replaced by Samuel A. Alito. Three liberal justices, David Souter, John Paul Stevens, and Ruth Bader Ginsberg, may retire in the near future. The Court could turn dramatically toward Thomas's strong conservative views if a Republican president nominates conservative replacements. If a Democratic president names new justices, the Court's makeup may stay the same. Whether he wants to be or not, Clarence Thomas is the most famous justice of the current Supreme Court. His color, his confirmation, and his voting record keep him that way.

He describes himself in his autobiography as "an ordinary man to whom extraordinary things happened." Indeed, Thomas rose out of a period of great injustice to become a Supreme Court justice. He is a man of many temperaments. On one hand, he blasts his critics with fiery indignation that still smolders from the past. On the other hand, he inspires great affection from those who experience the warmth and enthusiasm of his off-bench personality. He has succeeded both because of, and in spite of, his color, yet, he is a black man who wants the law and his life to be color blind. If he is silent, he is criticized. If he expresses his views, he is criticized.

In the end, none of it matters very much. Thomas may stay on the Supreme Court as long as he wants to—even for the rest of his life. That could be a very long time.

According to Lawrence Baum, Thomas told two of his law clerks that he may remain on the Court until 2034. "The liberals made my life miserable for 43 years, and I'm going to make their lives miserable for 43 years." He has already served on the bench longer than the average Supreme Court justice. He could become one of the longest-serving justices ever, if not the longest serving. If that is the case, Thomas can go to sleep smiling. The controversy and difficulties that have laced his rise to the highest court in the land will mean nothing. His big booming voice can echo through the Court's marble halls, his last and best laugh yet.

1948   Clarence Thomas is born in Pin Point, Georgia, on June 23.

1954   Clarence enrolls in segregated Haven Home School.

1955   Clarence and his brother go to live with Myers and Tina Anderson, their grandparents; Clarence enrolls in St. Benedict the Moor School in Savannah.

1957   Clarence and Myers help their grandfather build a house on his Liberty County farm.

1962   Clarence graduates from St. Benedict's and enters St. Pius X High School.

1964   He enters St. John Vianney Minor Seminary.

1967   Thomas graduates from St. John's and enrolls in Immaculate Conception Seminary in northwestern Missouri.

1968   He drops out of Immaculate Conception Seminary and enrolls in College of the Holy Cross.

1971   Thomas graduates from College of the Holy Cross; he marries Kathy Ambush.

1973   His son, Jamal Adeen, is born.

1974   Thomas graduates from Yale Law School on May 20; he is admitted to the Missouri Bar; he works for Missouri Attorney General John C. Danforth.

1976   Thomas joins Monsanto Chemical Company in St. Louis.

1979   He joins the staff of Senator Danforth as a legislative assistant.

1980   He registers as a Republican.

1981   Thomas becomes assistant secretary for civil rights in the U.S. Department of Education.

1982   He is named chairman of the Equal Employment Opportunity Commission (EEOC).

1983 Myers Anderson, Thomas's grandfather, and Tina Anderson, his grandmother, die.

1984 Clarence and Kathy Thomas divorce; Thomas takes custody of Jamal.

1987 Thomas marries Virginia Lamp in Omaha, Nebraska.

1989 On March 12, Thomas is appointed judge of the U.S. Court of Appeals for the District of Columbia.

1991 Justice Thurgood Marshall announces his retirement on June 27; President Bush nominates Thomas to replace Marshall on the Supreme Court on July 1; confirmation hearings begin before the Senate Judiciary Committee on September 10; the committee votes 7–7 on confirmation on September 27; hearings reopen to consider Anita Hill's sexual harassment charges on October 11; the Senate confirms Thomas by a vote of 52–48 on October 15; Thomas is sworn in as the one-hundred-sixth justice of the Supreme Court on October 23.

1997 The Thomases adopt Marky Martin.

2007 Thomas publishes his autobiography, *My Grandfather's Son*.

Foskett, Ken. *Judging Thomas: The Life and Times of Clarence Thomas.* New York: HarperCollins, 2004.

Halliburton, Warren J. *Clarence Thomas: Supreme Court Justice.* Hillside, N.J.: Enslow Publishers, 1993.

Haskins, Jim. *Separate But Not Equal: The Dream and the Struggle.* New York: Scholastic Press, 1998.

Hurley, Jennifer A. *Racism.* San Diego: Greenhaven Press, 1998.

Merida, Kevin, and Michael Fletcher. *Supreme Discomfort: The Divided Soul of Clarence Thomas.* New York: Doubleday, 2007.

Morrison, Toni. *Remember: The Journey to School Integration.* Boston: Houghton Mifflin, 2004.

Pederson, William D., and Norman W. Provizer, editors. *Great Justices of the U.S. Supreme Court.* New York: Peter Lang, 1994.

Toobin, Jeffrey. *The Nine: Inside the Secret World of the Supreme Court.* New York: Doubleday, 2007.

Wagman, Robert I. *The Supreme Court: A Citizen's Guide.* New York: Pharos Books, 1993.

Wagner, Heather Lehr. *The Supreme Court.* New York: Chelsea House Publishers, 2007.

Williams, Mary E. *Interracial America.* San Diego: Greenhaven Press, 2001.

WEB SITES
"Clarence Thomas," The Supreme Court Historical Society
http://www.supremecourthistory.org/myweb/justice/thomas.htm

"The Court Defines Itself. *Marbury v. Madison*," History of the Supreme Court
http://www.historyofsupremecourt.org/history/defines/opener.htm

History of the Supreme Court
http://www.historyofsupremecourt.org/overview.htm

Picture Credits

Vicki Cox has written 11 children's books. She writes for national magazines and newspapers in 16 states. She has an M.S. in education and taught in the public school system for 25 years. She lives in Lebanon, Missouri, and Oak Park, Illinois.